SEEKING FREEDOM

A History of the Underground Railroad in Howard County, Maryland

The Howard County
Center of
African American
Culture, Inc.
is proud to
dedicate this
publication to
Paulina Cooper Moss

SEEKING FREEDOM

A History of the Underground Railroad in Howard County, Maryland

Edited by
Paulina C. Moss
and
Levirn Hill

With the assistance of
Laurence Hurst
Virginia C. Lee
Wylene S. Burch

Historical Consultant
Joetta Cramm

Grateful acknowledgement is made to the
Columbia Foundation, Inc. and the
Maryland Historical Trust for the financial assistance
with the publication of this work.

Some Dates in the History of Howard County

1687	First original land grant in what was then known as Upper Anne Arundel (now Howard County).
1700	Elkridge Landing is a seaport rivaling Annapolis. It is established as a town in 1734.
1772	The Ellicott Brothers, Joseph, Andrew and John, arrive from Bucks County, Pennsylvania, to establish mills along the Patapsco River. The settlement of Ellicott's Mills begins.
1776	Charles Carroll, residing at Doughoregan Manor in Howard County, signs the Declaration of Independence for Maryland.
1831	The first railroad station in America is built at Ellicott's Mills.
1831	Peter Cooper's "Tom Thumb" initiates the use of steam power at the B&O Station in Ellicott's Mills, and America's Railroad Age begins.
1851	Howard becomes a separate county with the county seat at Ellicott's Mills, where the present courthouse had been built in 1843.
1862	Howard County is the scene of a Civil War episode in which the Winans Steam Gun is captured. Federal troops are stationed at Relay.
1878	The Hopkins Atlas maps the county's six districts and identifies landowners.
1962	The Centennial of the Civil War is observed with the re-enactment of the Steam Gun episode, a ball, and other events.
1967	Columbia, the "new town" conceived by James Rouse, is established, occupying large areas of the county.
1968	The county, which had been governed by a Board of Commissioners, adopts the charter form of government with a County Executive and County Council.
1972	Ellicott City celebrates its Bicentennial with a pageant, parade, and other events. The Ellicotts, Benjamin Banneker, and Charles Carroll are among those depicted.
1978	The Ellicott City Historic District is placed on the National Register of Historic Places. Twenty-five other sites in the county have been so designated.

SEEKING FREEDOM   v

FOREWORD

Writing the story of the Underground Railroad in Howard County was spearheaded by Paulina Moss, who was a volunteer researcher at the Howard County Center of African American Culture, Inc., until her death in November, 1999. Paulina, along with me, the Director, spent four years traveling the highways and byways of Howard County, investigating and researching sources that would document the route of the Underground Railroad. Endless hours of written research and countless oral interviews helped us put the pieces of this story together. The long-untold history of the UGR in Howard County could now be told.

As we walked through two centuries of the history of Howard County history, we began to see that freedom was taken from people of African descent. Yet, as the story unfolded, we saw how people of diverse racial and religious backgrounds worked together to free those in bondage. Howard County's story provided a glimpse into the inner life of Blacks in bondage. This story introduced us to people who showed compassion and concern for others, at the risk of their own lives.

Paulina wanted all to know that the contributions made by African Americans were firmly embedded in the history of Howard County. She wanted to tell the African American experience that helped to shape, mold, enrich, and give character to the county. She expressed with boldness and assurance that the information gathered was historically correct. Committed to youth, Paulina wanted them to understand that despite the hardships, while under bondage, African Americans of Howard County triumphed leaving a heritage of significant contributions.

Wylene S. Burch, Director

On the Road To Freedom...

Paulina C. Moss and Wylene S. Burch
retrace routes on the Underground Railroad in
Howard County, Maryland

ACKNOWLEDGEMENTS

The Board and Staff of the Howard County Center of African American Culture, Inc. (HCCAAC) wish to express deep gratitude to the many individuals who participated in the development of this Underground Railroad Project, *Seeking Freedom: A History of the Underground Railroad in Howard County, Maryland.* Their collective efforts reflect a singleness of purpose and an undying love for the glorious history that include the contributions of African Americans in Howard County. We extend our sincerest thanks to all those who helped to make this publication possible.

Our debt is deepest to all the persons interviewed for this publication. They unselfishly gave of their time and shared their history; each helped to fill in gaps in our knowledge of the story. They took us to places we have never been in mind or body. They enriched our understanding of the past and deepened our appreciation of the many ways America and the world owe a debt of gratitude to the conductors and contributors of the Underground Railroad.

Our heartfelt gratitude goes to Paulina Moss who spent countless hours researching, documenting, and developing the ideas and concepts presented. Paulina Moss and Peg Cunningham both gave careful attention to the details that crafted the manuscript. Wylene Burch developed the core of the research essential to the book's progress by providing editing, field studies, research and overall assistance. For their research and contributions on the history of slavery in Howard County, we acknowledge Judi Cephas, Julie DeMatteis, Karla Killian (student of Atholton High School), Roland Howard, Gloria Kisner, Kimberly Lockhart and Maurine McKinley.

Laurence Hurst provided editorial assistance and he shared scholarly research that helped develop an authentic narrative. Historian Beulah Buckner provided referenced insights into many sensitive local issues. Paulina Moss, Gloria Kisner, and Marian Jackson recorded and developed biographical highlights of native Howard Countians over the age of eighty. Laurence Hurst developed the oral history interviews with the assistance of Marilyn Miles and Jacqueline Lipscomb. Remus Lyles contributed information and documentation of four generations of family history in Howard County. Virginia Lee helped edit the craft and provided clarification of the story's direction. Brandon Noble aided Paulina Moss in selecting graphic materials. Laurence Hurst with Wylene Burch selected the photographs and developed text of historical homes and residents. We gratefully acknowledge Vera Wilson and Octavia Carter for proofreading the final manuscript and Levirn Hill for assuming the role as editor of this work upon the death of Paulina Moss.

We thank all persons who encouraged HCCAAC to undertake this project to give a voice to an untold history. Finally, we thank Anthony Cohen who documented and wrote the history of the *Underground Railroad in Montgomery County* and who served as a mentor in helping us unravel the story of the Underground Railroad here in Howard County.

This project was made possible by the State of Maryland, Maryland Department of Housing and Community Development, Maryland Historical Trust, Maryland State Archives, Howard County Historical Society, University of Maryland Baltimore County Library (Archival Department), Columbia Foundation, Library of Congress, Howard County Center of African American Culture, Inc., and Preservation Howard County. Photographs courtesy of the Maryland Historical Trust are by Cleora Thompson, David W. Donoho, Jean Ewing, and E.A. Masek, Jr. Other photograph credits go to Laurence Hurst, J.M. Eddins, Jr., Doug Kapustin, Jason Lee, Larry Crouse, Michael Hayes, Olan Mills, Jacqualine Streeter, James C. Wilfong, Jr., Amy Worden, and *The Sun* in Howard County.

Willis E. Gay, Chairman
HCCAAC Board of Directors

ACKNOWLEDGEMENTS ix

INTRODUCTION

In 1996, the Howard County Center of African American Culture, Inc., (HCCAAC), began researching and recording the history of the Underground Railroad (UGR) in Howard County, Maryland. The undertaking began after learning of an UGR project completed in Montgomery County, Maryland by Anthony Cohen and the American Friends Service Committee. Cohen was successful in identifying and recording in a published document the history of the Underground Railroad in Montgomery County.

Anthony Cohen met with the volunteers from HCCAAC who were interested in completing a similar project on Howard County. Cohen was informed that there was already knowledge that Harriet Tubman had led enslaved African Americans through the Simpsonville and Elkridge areas. Upon learning of the UGR movement in the county, Cohen again met with volunteers and Wylene Burch (Founder and Director of HCCAAC) to discuss undertaking the project. It was decided that HCCAAC would indeed research and record for publication the history of the UGR in Howard County. The group also decided that HCCAAC would petition the county to serve as the designated site for the study. These efforts are ongoing. Volunteers included Paulina Moss, Beulah Buckner, Gloria Kisner, Phyllis Knill, Kimberly Lockhart, Angela Stevens, Anita Stewart, Julie DeMatteis, Lee Preston, Judi Cephas and Constance Allen.

HCCAAC volunteers held several meetings with Cohen, during which he explained where and how to gather facts and other information for the project. He recommended reviews of census, state archival, cemetery, and church records; library references; and conducting oral interviews. During the research phase, this information proved invaluable. Additional documents were located at the Maryland Historical Library in Crownsville, Maryland, the State Archives in Annapolis and the Howard County Historical Society.

Seeking Freedom: A History of the Underground Railroad in Howard County, Maryland includes Parts I, II, and III. Part I of the text gives a brief history of the emergence of slavery in Maryland. It takes a brief look at slavery in Howard County and concludes with a look at early Columbia, Maryland and Columbia, a planned community. Part II of the text provides a pictorial tour of several plantation houses. Part III gives a bird's eye view of the route of the Underground Railroad in the county. The Conclusion provides recommendations for keeping the story of the Underground Railroad in the county alive. This publication features biographical highlights of senior Howard Countians who provided a picture of life in the county for African Americans fifty years after slavery and concludes with a selection of oral interviews. A bibliography is provided for further study.

The history of African Americans seeking freedom is one of courage, strength and persistence. It also is a story of cooperation between blacks and whites from different religious and cultural backgrounds. Our goal in recording this story is keeping the history of the Underground Railroad alive. We also want to highlight the important role African Americans played in this movement and in the history of the United States. Moreover, we hope the UGR story will serve to enlighten the reader on how people of different persuasions and viewpoints can work for a common cause and outcome – freedom and the uplifting of human beings, everywhere.

Virginia C. Lee, Vice-Chairperson
HCCAAC Board of Directors

Table of Contents

Foreword vi
Acknowledgements viii
Introduction x

Part I
A. Emergence of Slavery in Maryland 2
B. Slavery in Howard County 16
C. Early Columbia and Columbia, a Planned Community 28

Part II
Underground Railroad Stops in Howard County 32

Part III
Plantation Houses in Howard County 52
    Clarksville 54
    Columbia 56
    Cooksville 61
    Daisy 62
    Elkridge 63
    Ellicott City 66
    Glenelg 72
    Glenwood 74
    Highland 76
    Laurel (North) 77
    Lisbon 78
    Marriottsville 79
    Sykesville 81
    Woodbine 82
Biographical Highlights 86
Oral History 98
Conclusion 112
Bibliography 114

PART I
Section A

Emergence of Slavery in Maryland

Historical Chronology of Maryland

1632	Maryland Charter granted to Cecil Calvert, 2nd Lord Baltimore
1634	First blacks, John Price and Matthias de Sousa, arrive in Maryland
1664	Slavery sanctioned by law, slaves to serve for life
1774	Pennsylvania Society for Promoting the Abolition of Slavery established
1789	Maryland Society for the Abolition of Slavery established
1810	Free blacks disenfranchised
1850	Fugitive Slave Law passed
1859	John Brown from Maryland launched raid on Harper's Ferry
1864	Maryland slaves emancipated by State Constitution on November 1

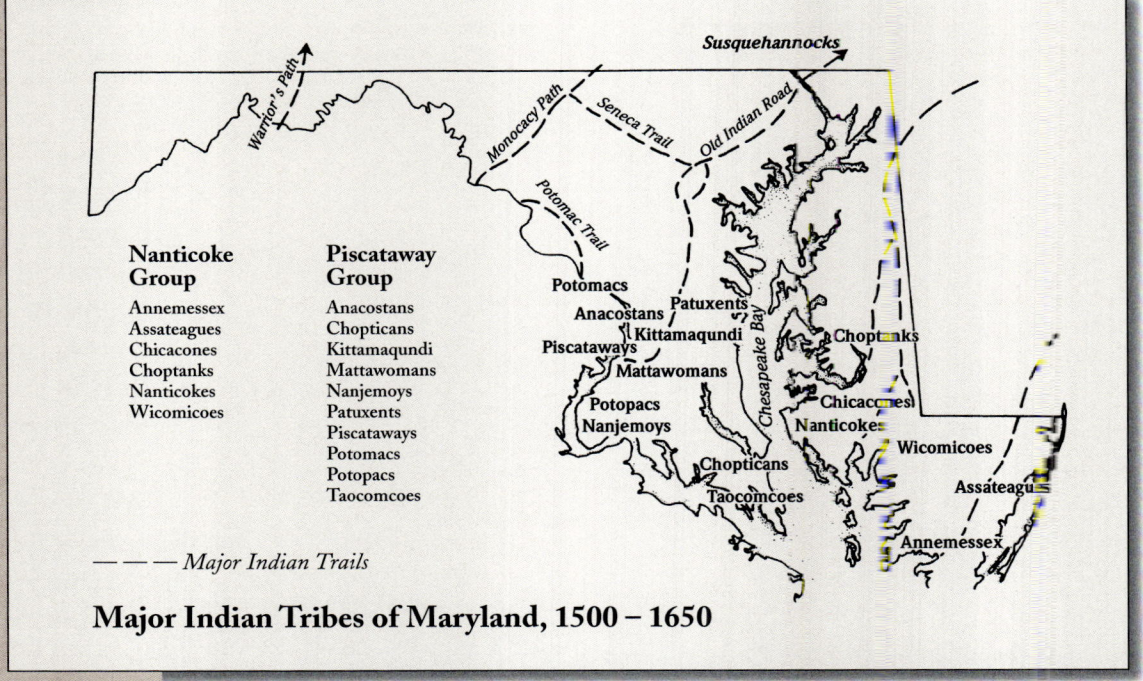

Major Indian Tribes of Maryland, 1500 – 1650

2 SEEKING FREEDOM

Introduction

There were many Indian tribes in Maryland before colonists arrived. These Native Americans had lived in Maryland for over 10,000 years. "By or about 1700, Maryland's Indian population had been killed off or pushed Westward."[1] The disenfranchisement of the Indian, which made colonization possible, is often lost in the telling of American history.

The Underground Railroad (UGR) is another story often lost in the telling of history in America. It is the story of slavery as an institution and the heroic resistance to it. Information researched and documented concerning the UGR in Howard County, Maryland, covers just a few miles on the long journey of the Underground Movement. It is hoped that it adds to the growing tracts in the long overdue story of the Underground Railroad.

Maryland Established

On June 20, 1632, a Maryland Charter was granted to Cecil Calvert, 2nd Lord Baltimore, by Charles I, King of Great Britain and Ireland. Two ships set sail from Cowes, England to establish the colony which later became Maryland. After the Revolutionary War of 1776, Maryland became independent of Great Britain. Maryland became one of the thirteen original states in the Union.

From its beginning, the state of Maryland benefited from the generosity of Lord Baltimore who granted large tracts of land to the settlers in exchange for quit rents paid twice yearly. The basic commercial crop for the agricultural system of the state was tobacco. "This initial cash crop played an important role in the economic and political growth of the colony."[2]

First African Americans Arrived in Maryland

In 1634, two small ships, the Ark and the Dove from Cowes, England landed at St. Clements Island in Maryland. Among the first settlers of Maryland were two men known to be of African descent— John Price and Matthias de Sousa. Price arrived on the Dove and Matthias de Sousa arrived on the Ark. Like many of the whites, both Price and de Sousa had no money to pay for their voyage, so they agreed to work for up to seven years to repay their debt.

Little could be found about John Price; however, records show that Matthias de Sousa paid his debt and gained his freedom. He became a captain of a sailboat that explored Maryland waters and traded with many Indian tribes.[3] Being privileged as one of the first free blacks in the state, Matthias perhaps witnessed the emergence of slavery and treasured his freedom.

Public notice of an estate sale.

Emergence of Slavery in Maryland

As early as 1638, reference was made to slaves in an Act of the Maryland Legislature.

> Be it enacted by the lord proprietor of this province
> of and with advice and approbation of
> the freemen of the same
> that all persons being Christians (slaves excepted)
> of the age of eighteen years
> or above brought into this province
> at the charge and adventure of some other person
> shall serve such person...
> for the full term of four years.[4]

This act of legislation guaranteed that indentured servants brought to the colonies to work the land would complete their term of four years. Prior to 1700, planters brought white indentured servants as laborers at a rate of $950 annually, but they were found to be unsuitable for the grueling work required on a tobacco farm and far too costly. After 1700, enslaved Africans, who could best tolerate the heat, began arriving in increasing numbers. According to the census report of 1704, the African (Negro) population was 4,475; by 1720 it had reached 25,000. This increase in the Negro population required less importation of white indentured servants. During this period, Maryland was recognized as a leading slave-holding state with a significant African American population, both free and enslaved.

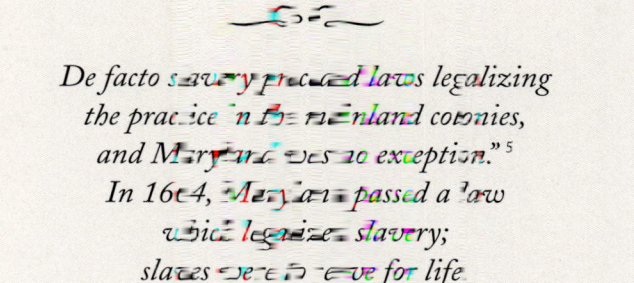

> De facto slavery preceded laws legalizing
> the practice in the mainland colonies,
> and Maryland was no exception."[5]
> In 1664, Maryland passed a law
> which legalized slavery;
> slaves were to serve for life.

The economic prosperity produced by the tobacco industry and the free labor of slaves produced a class of landed gentry and affluent elite. These included squires who became delegates in the Assembly, justices for the county court system, vestrymen in parishes, and officers for the militia. They formed a powerful elite that continued throughout the period of enforced slavery. This powerful elite came to realize that to sustain their way of life they needed even more labor to produce the volume of tobacco requested by their British buyers. They also realized that the institution of slavery had to be preserved at all costs. The merchant planters of the state even saw the selling of slaves as a lucrative extension of the tobacco business. Between 1760 and 1780, the population of Maryland increased by 53,207 and set the population at 245,474. Of the increase, 31,512 were African Americans destined to work the tobacco fields.

The government accepted slavery as an institution that affected the free black population as well. Rapid growth of this segment of the population in the early 1800's produced a ratio of three enslaved persons to every one free black person. Several restrictions, fashioned to dehumanize the free black population, were meant to establish them as "second class citizens," therefore making them inferior to whites. Here we find the heroes of our history in the population of the free black persons of whom so little is known.

The rod was seldom spared in the daily life on plantations or in the homes of slaveowners.

Frederick Douglass
Circa 1868
Etching Engraved by A.H. Ritchie
Collection: HCCAAC

We do know they spoke about their disenfranchisement and acted diligently to emphasize their rights as human beings. Their resiliency and resourcefulness allowed them to develop religious and social organizations, promote education, and purchase real estate. However, by 1810 free blacks were still deprived of many rights in Maryland.[4]

In the nineteenth century, the majority of enslaved persons were engaged in agricultural field work. Others labored as artisans, wagon and barrel makers, smiths, stone cutters, and harness workers. Still others worked in shipbuilding and as craftsmen and warehousemen. The women created clothing for daily wear on the plantations, made quilts and linens for the main house, prepared and preserved food stock or performed any other task the mistress or master deemed necessary.

The Beginning of the Underground Railroad in Maryland

During periods of economic depression, the enslaved population suffered harsher treatment. Demands were placed on them to increase their work output dramatically. Some owners tried successfully to hire their slaves out as additional sources of income.

Life on plantations varied, depending on the character of the owners. "Some enslaved persons received severe whippings lasting until the abused person collapsed." Frederick Douglass, a native of Maryland, attributed his lack of contact with his mother as a "rule of the master." It was his master's desire to dehumanize the person, or persons, being abused."[6]

Slaves, tired of bondage and abuse, began to risk their lives for freedom by escaping. The increased number of runaway slaves resulted in establishing slave patrols to halt the frequency of escape, or attempted escapes. The increased number of runaway slaves also resulted in the organization of the Maryland Colonization Society that sought the removal of persons from the state, promoting a return to Africa. The Society's viewpoint was strongly condemned by the leaders of the day, who were in favor of the cessation of slavery. A mass meeting of black people in New York City in the 1830's attacked the plan and attitude of the American Colonization Society.[7] To curtail the increase in runaways, the Fugitive Slave Law was passed in 1850. The law forced northern states to return runaway slaves to their southern owners.

In 1852, 41 freed blacks went to the state convention in Annapolis, Maryland to protest their conditions and that of slaves. They convened despite laws that forbade them to organize and have meetings. Freed blacks played a critical role in assisting slaves in escaping from bondage.

It is reported that the consciences of many Marylanders, particularly members of the Society of Friends (Quakers), caused them to petition for the abolition of slavery. Quakers are reported to have been major supporters of the Underground Railroad Movement in Maryland and Pennsylvania. In 1774, the Pennsylvania Society for Promoting the Abolition of Slavery was established. Between 1787–1788, six Marylanders were members of the Pennsylvania Society. In 1787, Luther Martin appealed to Constitutional Congress to stop slavery. That same year, 1787, Baltimore Quakers (Friends) petitioned for the abolition of slavery. In 1789, the Maryland Society to Abolish Slavery was established. "The Maryland Society petitioned the assembly to extend rights guaranteed in the Declaration of Independence and the Constitution to African Americans and, in the state courts, entered lawsuits, (Freedom Suits) on behalf of some slaves."[8] That same year, a Maryland Senate Bill was introduced. Many homes of these Quakers were used to assist fugitives attempting to escape to freedom.

So how did those who had been denied their freedom and those who recognized the heinous act of slavery proceed? An Underground Railroad system was devised throughout the southern states to assist slaves in escaping to freedom in the northern and western states and into Canada. The homes of antislavery sympathizers and freed blacks throughout Maryland provided safe havens for fugitives on the Underground Railroad.

As a border state, Maryland would play a pivotal role in the Underground Movement. It would serve as one of the last slave states many fugitives passed through to reach the free states of Pennsylvania to the north and Ohio to the west. Pennsylvania and Ohio were two of the most heavily traversed states on the Underground Railroad.

End of Slavery in Maryland

In the United States, antislavery activity began in colonial days. There were distinct forces that played a part in the end of slavery in Maryland and the United States.

"During the 1680's, Quakers in Pennsylvania condemned slavery on moral grounds. In the late 1700's several leaders of the American Revolution Movement including Thomas Jefferson and Patrick Henry spoke out against slavery."[9]

In 1789, Charles Carroll, a prominent member of the landed gentry in the state, introduced in the Maryland Senate a bill aimed at the gradual abolition of slavery in Maryland. He was a slave owner who had signed the Declaration of Independence. It is reported that he recognized the hypocrisy of his situation, having endorsed "that all men had the right to life, liberty, and the pursuit of happiness." At the time he was recognized as one of the largest slaveholders, with 150 persons being held in bondage on his estates.

"John Brown's Raid in 1859 sent waves of fear throughout Maryland. The Maryland Legislature, in turn, reacted in a negative manner by passing additional restrictive laws called *Black Codes* to insure the institution of slavery."[10]

Pro-slavery and anti-slavery forces clashed before and during the Civil War. "On the eve of the war, sensitivity to the slavery issue was

THOUGHTS FOR ALL TIME
by Frederick Douglass

*"I would unite with anybody to do right
And with nobody to do wrong."*

> **STEAL AWAY TO JESUS**
> (Slave Song)
>
> *Steal away, steal away, Steal away to Jesus:*
> *Steal away; steal away home.*
> *I ain't got long to stay here.*
>
> *My Lord calls me. He calls me by the thunder.*
> *The trumpet sounds within my soul.*
> *I ain't got long to stay here.*
>
> *Green trees abendin' Poor sinner stands a tremblin'.*
> *The trumpet sounds within my soul.*
> *I ain't got long to stay here.*
>
> *Steal away, steal away, Steal away to Jesus.*
> *Steal away, steal away home.*
> *I ain't got long to stay here.*
>
> Arr. by Work Brothers

at the boiling point. In late 1861, a General John A. Dix ordered that no slaves except laborers and servants who had the consent of their masters could enter military service."[11] The issue of slaves escaping became an even more serious issue for slave owners in Maryland. They expressed fear of the disastrous economic consequences that the massive loss of slave labor would have on their agricultural interests."[12]

In 1860, the value of enslaved persons in the state had been estimated at $35,331,111.00; by 1864, Samuel Harrison stated, "slavery (the institution) has become valueless."[13] On November 1, 1864, Maryland's slaves were emancipated by the state constitution. In 1865, the 13th Amendment to the U.S. Constitution abolished slavery in the country.

Types of Documents Found in the Maryland State Archives

MANUMISSIONS
A Manumission paper was a legal document that formally freed slaves. Between 1752 and 1790, the deed (also known as Manumission) was the only legal document that could free an enslaved person. But before 1752 and after 1790, manumissions were recorded in wills and chattel records. In 1805, a law requiring all free African Americans to secure a *Certificate of Freedom* was passed by the Maryland General Assembly. The law was enacted to identify this group of freed persons and record proof of identity in the county court.

TAX RECORDS
Maryland residents who held African American persons in bondage paid personal property taxes on each individual so enslaved.

CHATTEL RECORDS
These records were bills of sale for personal property, such as cattle, horses, tobacco and farm implements. Prior to the Civil War, the sale of persons as slaves was recorded in the Chattel Records.

RUNAWAY DOCKETS
If an enslaved person was suspected of being a runaway, and the court could not prove his or her status, the sheriff would hold the person involved and advertise him or her as a runaway in the newspapers. If there were no claim, the suspected runaway was set free. This law came into being in 1824 by the General Assembly, Chapter 171, Laws of 1824.

CENSUS RECORDS
An official enumeration of the population of a country and various statistics.

REWARD

RANAWAY from the subscriber, living near Annapolis, a mulatto slave named TONEY, a very likely, well made, active fellow, about twenty years old, five feet eight or nine inches high; had on when he went away, a felt hat bound round, osnabrig shirt and breeches, thread stockings, and black shoes with buckles, he has been a good deal used to horses, and is very handy; he will probably attempt to get to Baltimore and pass as a free man, from his colour. Whoever takes and secures the said fellow, so that his master gets him again, shall receive, if above ten miles from home thirty shillings, if out of the county forty shillings, and if out of this state the above reward, including what the law allows, paid by BRICE T.B. WORTHINGTON.

July 17, 1786
Maryland Gazette

THE STATE OF MARYLAND

ANNE ARUNDEL COUNTY, – to wit:

I HEREBY CERTIFY to all whom it doth or may concern, that on an examination of the Records and Papers in the Office of the **Register of Wills for Anne Arundel County**, it appears that the last will and testament of *Brice J.G. Worthington* late of the County aforesaid, deceased, – bearing date the *twentieth* day of *April* in the year of our Lord one thousand eight hundred and *twenty-six* was proved and recorded in the said office on the twenty-eighth day of November in the year of our Lord one thousand eight hundred and *twenty-six* in Liber *EV, IG* No. – – – folio *308* and that the said *Brice J.G. Worthington* by his said will, among other things did devise and direct that *all of his Negro slaves under the age of Thirty, they and their increase should be free at the age of Thirty years.*

AND I DO FURTHER CERTIFY, that it hath been proved by such testimony as is satisfactory to me, that the bearer hereof, Negro *Isaac* whose height is about five feet *six* inches: whose age is about *Thirty years* whose complexion is *Dark Chestnut* and who, as appears by the said will and testimony, became Free *on or about the fifteenth November Eighteen hundred and fifty nine (has a scar on forefinger...)* is the identical person who was Manumitted or Freed as aforesaid, — and that the said Negro *Isaac* was raised in *A.A. (now Howard) County.*

In Testimony Whereof, I hereunto subscribe my name, and affix the seal of my Office, this *Twentieth* day of *August* in the year of our Lord one thousand eight hundred and *sixty*.

TEST,

Benj E. Grantt
Register of Wills for Anne Arundel County.

Manumission of Isaac Worthington, November, 1859

SEEKING FREEDOM

PERSONAL

$50 REWARD — Left the Lombard Street Infirmary, (where he had been undergoing medical treatment,) on Wednesday the 24 inst. my NEGRO MAN HENRY JONES. He is a copper colored mulatto, 34 years old six feet high, slender and sickly looking; was dressed, when he left, in full cloth drab coat, and blue cotton pants. I will give $50 for the apprehension of said negro within the State or $150 out of the State, secured in jail or otherwise so that the subscriber may get him.

               WILLIAM CLARK, near Clarksville
                   Howard County, Md.

$200 REWARD

RANAWAY from Waverly, the residence of the late George Howard, NEGRO ELIAS WILLIAMS. Said negro is about 6 feet high, very dark, small eye, lids swollen, very polite when spoken to, is a blacksmith by trade. The above reward will be given if taken in or out of the State—Had on, when last seen, a drab cloth coat and pantaloons, but may have changed them. Has a free wife in Baltimore.

                     P. HOWARD
            Executor of the late Geo. Howard

$300 REWARD

RANAWAY on Saturday evening the 30th, from the subscriber living in Howard District near Poplar Spring, FOUR NEGRO MEN, viz: Archibald, Nelson, Abraham, and Alfred. Abraham and Alfred are the property of Mrs. Sarah Allender of this city, Archibald and Nelson are brothers and of dark complexion—the one about 21 years of age, the other about 22; Abraham is rather lighter than the others and Alfred darker than any of them; Abraham is about 21 and Alfred 18 years of age.—the latter two are also brothers. Archibald is about 6 feet high, Nelson 5 feet 6 inches, Abraham 5 feet 10 inches, and Alfred about 5 feet 4. They are supposed to be in company, as they left at the same time. Fifty dollars reward will be paid by the subscriber for the apprehension of Archibald and Nelson, and $100 each for the other two by the owner thereof if taken out of the State and $50 if taken in the State.

                  EDWARD BRIAN,
                  Poplar Spring

Negro Population, Slave And Free, At Each Census By Divisions: 1790–1860

Division/State	1860 Slave	1860 Free	1850 Slave	1850 Free	1840 Slave	1840 Free	1830 Slave	1830 Free
United States	3,953,060	488,070	3,204,313	434,495	2,487,355	386,293	2,009,043	319,599
Maryland	87,189	83,942	90,368	74,723	89,737	62,078	102,994	52,938

Division/State	1820 Slave	1820 Free	1810 Slave	1810 Free	1800 Slave	1800 Free	1790 Slave	1790 Free
United States	1,538,022	233,634	1,191,362	186,446	803,602	108,435	697,624	59,557
Maryland	107,397	39,730	111,502	33,927	105,635	19,587	103,036	8,043

STATISTICS

In 1867, the General Assembly passed a law of complaint regarding formerly enslaved persons. Under the Military of the country, a large number of enslaved persons, held by Marylanders, were induced to leave and enlist in the United States Military Service. The law pointed out that the Marylanders of subject had received "no compensation for their inconvenience" (Chapter 189, Laws of 1867). Their desire was that the federal government would compensate the "owners" for the "chattel" lost. In response, the General Assembly ordered that a listing be made of all slave owners and the enslaved who enlisted in the Union Army as of November 1, 1864.

MILITARY RECORDS

Military records would prove the existence of slavery in Maryland. It appears that the federal government never compensated the owners; but the records provide evidence of the enslaved persons and their "owners" at the time of emancipation. Such information also provides the names of the enslaved who enlisted in the Union Army.

MILITARY REFLECTED CHANGING STATUS OF AFRICAN AMERICANS

Of all areas of endeavor, the one that best illustrated the changing status of blacks in Howard County is the military service. In both the American Revolution and the Civil War, black soldiers from the Howard County area fought bravely for their country.

During the colonial period, it had been the practice to exclude blacks from military service because of the fear that black soldiers might lead a slave revolt. During the American Revolution, however, the need for soldiers was such that Maryland was forced to put this consideration aside. But, unlike the Revolution, where blacks were integrated into white units, the Civil War segregated black soldiers into their own regiments.

"Most of the blacks of Howard County went to Baltimore to enlist."[14] "Eighty-seven African American soldiers are listed on the Howard County Slave Ledger of 1864."[15]

U.S. Congressional Medal of Honor Recipient – Decatur Dorsey of Howard County

Decatur Dorsey, born 1836 in Anne Arundel County (now Howard County), entered the military from Baltimore County, Maryland on March 25, 1864. After nine months in Company B, 39th U.S. Colored Regiment, he was promoted to 1st Sergeant and became the first black soldier to receive the Congressional Medal of Honor for distinguished service. He planted the colors on the Confederate soil in advance of his regiment. For his bravery, he was awarded a Congressional Medal of Honor on November 8, 1865.[15] Decatur Dorsey married Mannie Christie in Baltimore, Maryland on January 4, 1866 and later resided in Hoboken, New Jersey.

U.S. Congressional Medal of Honor

Sergeant Decatur Dorsey, Medal of Honor Recipient, buried at the Flower Hill Cemetery in North Bergen, New Jersey.

EMERGENCE OF SLAVERY IN MARYLAND 13

"The old flag never touched the ground, boys."

– Sergeant William Carney,
U.S. Congressional Medal of Honor Recipient, USCT

Over 180,000 blacks served in the United States Colored Troops units, constituting 10% of the total Union strength.[17]

"Who would be free themselves must strike the blow.

Better even to die free than to live slaves."

– Frederick Douglass
March 2, 1863

Deed of Manumission for George France
January 22, 1864

DEED OF MANUMISSION AND RELEASE OF SERVICE.

Whereas my slave *George France* has enlisted in the service of the United States: now, in consideration thereof, I, *Andrew Mercer* of *Howard* county, State of *Maryland*, do hereby, in consideration of said enlistment, manumit, set free, and release the above-named *George France* from all service due me; his freedom to commence from the *22d January 1864*, the date of his enlistment as aforesaid in the *9th* Regiment of Colored Troops in the service of the United States. *Co 7*

Witness my hand and seal, this *fifteenth* day of *September*, 1864

Andrew Mercer of R. [SEAL]

WITNESS:

S. Sykes

Howard COUNTY,
State of *Maryland Sept 15th*, 1864.

Before me appeared this day *Andrew Mercer*, and acknowledged the above Deed of Manumission and Release of Service to be his free act and deed.

S. Sykes J.P.

Courtesy: Howard County Historical Society

References

1. "Middle Atlantic Region, Maryland the People," *Britannica, Macropedia*, Vol. 29, Pg. 291.

2. "When Tobacco Was Money – Maryland, Suburbs of D.C." (http://mdsuburbs.about.com/us/mdsuburbs/library/weekly/aa032696.htm)

3. Cole, Robert, *Black Marylanders: A History for Children*, (Illustrated by Laurence Hurst Maryland: Maryland Bi-Centennial Commission and Maryland Department of Economic and Community Development, 1970–72, Pg. 1

4. "Maryland Historical Chronology" 1800–1899, http://www.mdarchives.state.md.us/msa/mdmanual/glance/html/chron16.html, Pg. 1

5. Walsh & Fox, *Maryland, A History, 1632–1974*, Maryland: Maryland Historical Society, 1974, Pg. 226

6. Douglass, Frederick, *Life and Times of Frederick Douglass*, New York: Thomas Y. Crowell Company Publishers, 1955, Pg. 2

7. Walsh & Fox, Eds., *op. cit.* Maryland: Maryland Historical Society, Pg. 231.

8. Guy, Anita Aidt, "The Maryland Abolition Society and the Promotion of the Ideals of a New Nation," *Maryland Historical Magazine*, Vol. 84, No. 4, Winter 1989, Pg. 342

9. "The African American Journey: From Slavery to Freedom (Abolition Movement)," (http://www.Worldbook.com/fun/aajourney/html/bho-3.html), Pg. 3

10. Walsh & Fox, Eds., *Op., Cit.*, Pg. 351

11. *Ibid.*, Pg. 362

12. *Ibid.*, Pg. 363

13. *Ibid.*, Pg. 370

14. *Morgan, Michael, Howard Sun, 2/22/81, Pg. 9*

15. *Veteran Records U.S. Colored Troops*, National Archives, Washington, DC

16. Beluah Buckner, "U.S. Colored Troops, Civil War & Buffalo Soldiers from Howard County," Maryland Book: Ellicott City Colored School Restoration Project, Pg. 7.

17. Black soldiers pledge allegiance to the United States, Department of Defense illustration

PART I
Section B
Slavery in Howard County

Historical Chronology

1649	Anglo Saxons settle on Severn River
1652	Anne Arundel County established
1690	Slavery well established in Howard County (then Upper Anne Arundel County)
1776	Charles Carroll signs Declaration of Independence
1835	Thomas Viaduct was completed
1839	Howard District established as settlement of Anne Arundel County
1851	Howard County established
1860	Census list: 1,395 freed blacks; 2,862 slaves; 9,081 whites

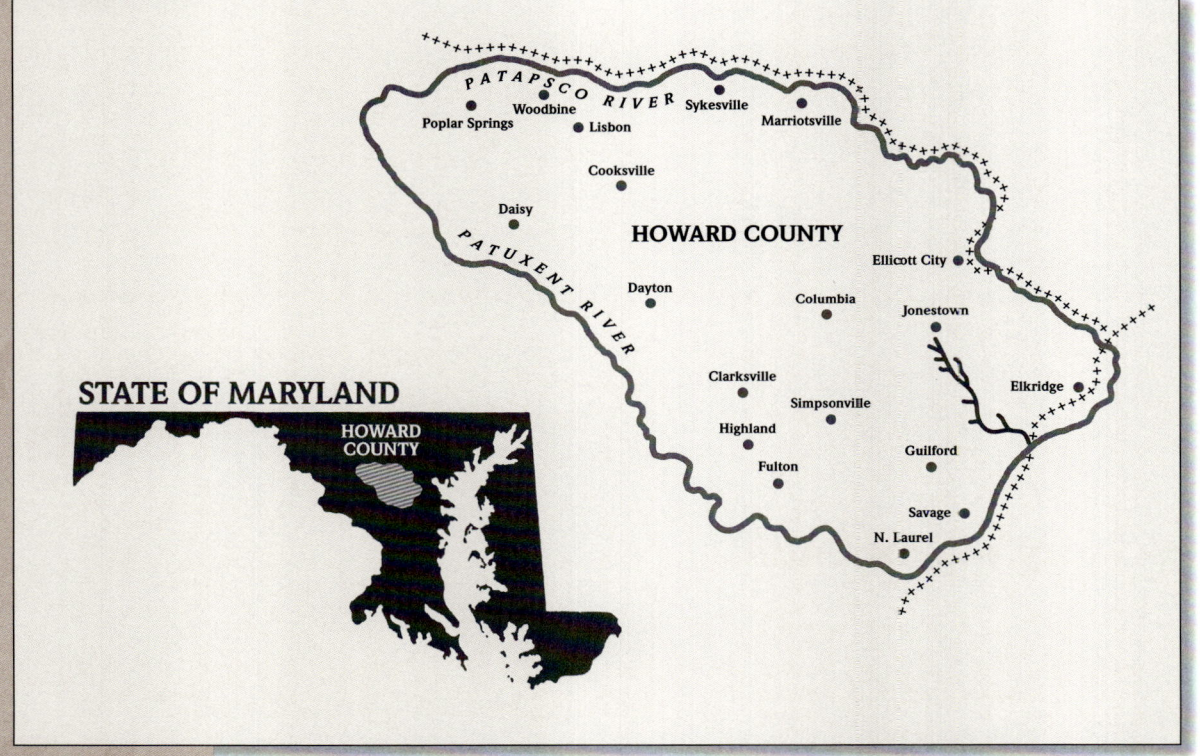

Howard County Established

In 1649, Anne Arundel County (part of what would become Howard County), was in its earliest stage of development. Its history dates back to the period when some of the first Anglo Saxons settled on the Severn River.

It was on July 30, 1650 that Governor William Stone visited the area in which the Puritans had settled and proclaimed the area Anne Arundel. In 1652, Anne Arundel County was officially established.

In 1839, Howard District was established as a settlement of Anne Arundel County. In 1851, Howard District separated from Anne Arundel County and became Howard County, becoming the 21st of Maryland's 23 counties. It was named after one of Maryland's most prominent citizens, John Eager Howard, a Revolutionary War hero, Governor of Maryland, and United States Senator.

Slavery in the County

Early colonists from England received land grants from the Lords Baltimore (Calvert Family) as inducements to locate here. Tobacco was the leading crop of Howard County during its early history. It was the first international trade product.

By 1690, slavery was well established in upper Anne Arundel County (now Howard County). Enslaved persons had begun to replace indentured servants. The institution of slavery, with its free labor force, made it possible for the cultivation of tobacco as the dominant moneymaker in all four geographic regions of the state. The enslavement of Africans provided free labor as an economical way to support the tobacco industry. This crop alone accelerated the economic development of the state and Anne Arundel County. The economic acceleration was primarily attributable to the unpaid labor of the enslaved.

The colonists came to realize that to sustain their way of life, they needed even more labor to dispense the volume of tobacco requested by their British buyers. To increase their labor pool, Maryland passed a law that disenfranchised many free blacks. "The census of 1860, the first taken after Howard separated from Anne Arundel, reported 68% of the population was white, 21.5% was slave and 10.5% were freed blacks. This compared with the overall population of Maryland at the time which was 75% white, 12.8% slaves and 12.2% free blacks. The total white population was only 9,081. In the first district of Howard County, 1,755 were white and 323 were free blacks. Prior to the Civil War the census did not enumerate slaves."[1]

1850 Federal Population Census #300 Slave Schedules

"Schedule of Slave Inhabitants in Howard District in the County of A. Arundel – State of Maryland enumerated by me on the 17th day of July, 1850, Geo. L. Stockett," Assistant Marshall

OWNER	DATE	MALE	FEMALE	CHILDREN	TOTAL
Benjamin Harrison	July 17, 1850	2	2	4	8
Benjamin Sunderland	July 17, 1850	2	0	4	6
Col. James Piper	July 17, 1850	3	2		5
Ellen A. Cooke	July 17, 1850	6	8	10	24
Evan Hughes	July 17, 1850	1	0	2	3
Henry H. Pare	July 17, 1850	2	0	2	4
Henry H. Pare	July 17, 1850	1	3	6	10
Isaac P. James	July 17, 1850	1	1		2
John D. Thomas	July 17, 1850	1	2	2	5
Ann Hunt	July 20 1850	0	0	1	1
Bernard U. Campbell	July 20 1850	0	0	1	1
Dudley Poor	July 20 1850	1	1	0	2
Elizabeth R. Ridgley	July 20 1850	1	4	12	17
Jane Scott	July 20 1850	0	1	0	1
Jesse Haynes	July 20 1850	1	2		3
Richard H. Waters	July 20 1850	0	0	1	1
Zachariah Mccauley	July 20 1850	1			1
Thomas I. Talbot	July 20 1850	4	2	4	10
Thomas Young	July 20 1850	1	1		2
William H. Mathews	July 20 1850	0	1		1
William S. Pamphilion	July 20 1850	0	1	0	1
George Worthington	July 20, 1850		1		1
George Dobbin	July 20, 1850	1			1
George Pocock	July 20, 1850		1		1
James Shipley	July 20, 1850	1			1
John Sewell	July 20, 1850		1	1	2
Joseph Pettitt	July 20, 1850		1		1
Rev. Richard Brown	July 20, 1850	5	5	1	11
Samuel Henry	July 20, 1850	1	1	1	3
Theodore Tubman	July 20, 1850	10	2	11	23
William Cecil	July 20, 1850	2	4	5	11
William Haynes	July 20, 1850	2	1	3	6
William Mills	July 20, 1850		1		1
Allen Dorsey	July 30, 1850	6	11	9	26
Charles G. Hanson	July 30, 1850	3	2	5	10
Dr. Allen Thomas	July 30, 1850	21	3	6	30
Rev. Richard Brown	July 30, 1850		1	12	13
Sarah Duborrow	July 30, 1850		1		1
William Knox	July 30, 1850		1	1	2
William Rowles	July 30, 1850		1	1	2
Amanda Green	August 9, 1850	1			1
Caroline B. Moore	August 9, 1850		2	5	7
Elizabeth Brown	August 9, 1850		1		1
Franklin F. James	August 9, 1850	1		1	2
Frederick Harmon	August 9, 1850			1	1
James Appleby	August 9, 1850				1
James Carn	August 9, 1850			1	1
Jeremiah Wells	August 9, 1850	1			1
John G. Holland	August 9, 1850		1	4	5
John P. Wall	August 9, 1850			1	1
Jonathan Waters	August 9, 1850	2	3	13	18
Joshua Anderson	August 9, 1850		1		1
Mary Bengu	August 9, 1850		1		1
Myers Pierce	August 9, 1850		1	3	4
Otho Belt	August 9, 1850	3			3
Rebecca Waters	August 9, 1850	1	1	3	5
Richard G. Watkins	August 9, 1850	1	2	1	4
Sarah Duborow	August 9, 1850			1	1
Septimus Hopkins	August 9, 1850	1	1	5	7
Thomas Watkins	August 9, 1850	1	2	7	10
William B. Dorsey	August 9, 1850	1	1	3	5
William Clark	August 9, 1850		1		1
William Cooke	August 9, 1850		1		1
William Haslup	August 9, 1850	2			2
Benjamin Williams	August 12, 1850		1		1
Charles G. Haslup	August 12, 1850			1	1

OWNER	DATE	MALE	FEMALE	CHILDREN	TOTAL
Charles Hammond	August 12, 1850	3	3	4	10
Dr. Michael Pue	August 12, 1850	2		3	6
George Hamilton	August 12, 1850	4	6	2	12
Hammond Dorsey	August 12, 1850	5	7	9	21
Henry McDade	August 12, 1850	1			1
Hetty C. Graham	August 12, 1850	1		1	3
Isaac Marc	August 12, 1850	6	3	6	15
Mary Hasko	August 12, 1850			1	1
Rebecca Dorsey	August 12, 1850			1	1
Rebecca Waters	August 12, 1850			3	3
William King	August 12, 1850		1	2	3
Mary P. Dorsey	August 15, 1850	5	2	5	12
Amon Laroay	August 20, 1850		1		1
Elizabeth Brown	August 20, 1850	3	2	9	14
Jane Clark	August 20, 1850	1			1
Sarah Childress	August 20, 1850			1	1
Zachariah Harden	August 20, 1850	3	1	4	8
Zedekiah Moore	August 20, 1850	3	2	6	13
Amos Welch	August 22, 1850			2	2
Deborah Disney	August 22, 1850			5	5
Eleanor Williams	August 22, 1850	2	2	5	9
Ezikiel Mills	August 22, 1850		1	2	3
Isaiah Mercer	August 22, 1850		1		1
James Clark	August 22, 1850	2		4	6
James Moore	August 22, 1850			1	1
Jeremiah Berry	August 22, 1850		8	5	13
Joel Blue	August 22, 1850	1		4	5
John R. Broom	August 22, 1850	2	1	1	4
John Warfield Of Losh	August 22, 1850	3	4	4	11
Osborne Conway	August 22, 1850	1		5	6
Peter Gormen	August 22, 1850	1	1		2
Richard Nels Gunn	August 22, 1850	1		5	6
Robert P. Dustin	August 22, 1850			1	1
William Lord	August 22, 1850			1	12
William M. Davis	August 22, 1850	1	1	2	4
Anna M. Hopkins	August 25, 1850	1	1	1	3
Anthony Smith	August 25, 1850	2	2	3	7

OWNER	DATE	MALE	FEMALE	CHILDREN	TOTAL
Catherine M. Rivers	August 25, 1850		1		1
Charles Brown	August 25, 1850	1	2	5	8
Christopher Harris	August 25, 1850			1	1
Edward C. Lyons	August 25, 1850		1		1
Elizabeth H. Hayden	August 25, 1850	1			1
Jacob Timanus	August 25, 1850			1	1
John Day	August 25, 1850			1	1
John L. Tyson	August 25, 1850			1	1
John T.B. Dorsey	August 25, 1850	1		1	2
John P. Carter	August 25, 1850	1	2		3
Malon Faulkner	August 25, 1850			1	1
Mary Gantt	August 25, 1850	1	1	2	4
Mclane Brown	August 25, 1850	1	1	2	4
Nickolas I. Barrett	August 25, 1850		2		2
Oliver Tagewell	August 25, 1850		1		1
Richard Iglehart	August 25, 1850	5	3	3	11
Samuel R. Powell	August 25, 1850	1			1
Stephen Hildebrand	August 25, 1850	1			1
Zedekiah M. Isaacs	August 25, 1850			1	1
Thomas Isaacs	August 25, 1850			1	1
Thomas Jenkins	August 25, 1850		1		2
Thomas Watkins	August 25, 1850	1			1
Alexander Haulkman	September 0, 1850		1		1
Arthur Pue	September 0, 1850	11	8	11	30
Charles N. Dorsey	September 0, 1850	11	7	10	28
George Ellicott	September 0, 1850			2	2
James B. Brooks	September 0, 1850	3	3	2	8
Thomas W. Ligon	September 0, 1850	3	2	5	10
Caleb Dorsey	September 1, 1850	13	5	9	28
John L.W. Dorsey	September 1, 1850	7	6	29	42
Robert H. Hare	September 1, 1850	5	2	2	9
Samuel D. Rogers	September 1, 1850	3	4	7	14
William Hughes	September 1, 1850			1	1
Freebon Hipsley	September 3, 1850	1	1	3	5
George Strichicomb	September 3, 1850	3	1		4
Nancy Fox	September 3, 1850	1	2	3	6
Reuben M. Dorsey	September 3, 1850	13	1	24	38

SLAVERY IN HOWARD COUNTY 19

OWNER	DATE	MALE	FEMALE	CHILDREN	TOTAL
Richard Davis	September 13, 1850	1	1	5	7
William Frost	September 13, 1850	5	4	5	14
William Hollifield	September 13, 1850			1	1
William Mcbee	September 13, 1850			2	2
William Fairale	September 13, 1850	1	2	4	7
Edward Hammond	September 19, 1850	1	5	9	15
Luther Welsh	September 19, 1850	1		1	2
Reuben	September 19, 1850	3	25		28
Thomas Dorsey	September 19, 1850	15	15	16	46
Charles Carroll	September 23, 1850	28	23	26	77
Charles Carroll	September 23, 1850	21	25	38	84
Benjamin West	October 1, 1850	1	1	2	4
Charles Carroll	October 1, 1850	5	3	4	12
Cornelius Hobbs	October 1, 1850			1	1
George R. Gaither	October 1, 1850	17	4	11	32
Henry W. Hood	October 1, 1850	3	3	1	7
Joel Iglehart	October 1, 1850			1	1
Luther Dorsey	October 1, 1850		1	1	2
Mathias Hammond	October 1, 1850	3	1	5	9
Richard Gambrile	October 1, 1850		1		1
Thaddeus L. Clark	October 1, 1850	3	1	4	8
Alexander Hammond	October 5, 1850	2	1		3
Amos Dorsey	October 5, 1850	2	4	6	12
Charles G. Ridgely, Jr.	October 5, 1850	1		3	4
Charles R. Simpson	October 5, 1850	2	1	5	8
Elizabeth Dean	October 5, 1850	1	2		3
George Bond	October 5, 1850	1	1	3	5
H. Linthicum	October 5, 1850	2		2	4
Isabella Crawford	October 5, 1850	4	3	11	18
Michael Dorsey	October 5, 1850	1		1	2
Nelson Phelp	October 5, 1850			4	4
Nelson Phelps	October 5, 1850	1	5	6	12
Nicholas Harding	October 5, 1850		2	2	4
Patrick Durming	October 5, 1850			3	3
S. Linthicum	October 5, 1850	3	1	1	5
Samuel L. Dorsey	October 5, 1850	1	2	4	7
T. Jones	October 5, 1850		1	1	2

OWNER	DATE	MALE	FEMALE	CHILDREN	TOTAL
Charles C. Ridgely	October 10, 1850	3	2	3	8
Denton Iglehart	October 10, 1850		1	1	2
Denton Miller	October 10, 1850	2	2	5	9
George Bradford	October 10, 1850	1		4	5
Harriet Iglehart	October 10, 1850	1	1	1	3
Henry H. Owings	October 10, 1850	2	1	4	7
Henry Warfield	October 10, 1850	2	2	3	7
James Clark	October 10, 1850	1	1	5	7
Lewis Carr	October 10, 1850		2	1	3
Lott Nicholson	October 10, 1850			1	1
Polly Welling	October 10, 1850	2	4	6	12
Richard Warfield	October 10, 1850	1	1		2
Samuel Waters	October 10, 1850	1		6	7
Sarah Welling	October 10, 1850	4	1	1	6
Thomas R. Hobbs	October 10, 1850			1	1
William Welling	October 10, 1850	1	1	5	7
Alfred Scaggs	October 15, 1850	2	2	3	7
Andrew I. Adams	October 15, 1850	3	2	4	9
Charles Carr	October 15, 1850	2	5	1	8
Elizabeth Wilson	October 15, 1850		1		1
Henry Melling	October 15, 1850		1	5	6
James Morris	October 15, 1850	1	2	2	5
James Walters	October 15, 1850	1	1	4	6
John Brown	October 15, 1850		1		1
John Cole	October 15, 1850	3	1		4
John R. Moore	October 15, 1850	2			2
Levi Young	October 15, 1850	2	1	5	8
Lorenza D. Wilson	October 15, 1850		4	3	7
Mary Adams	October 15, 1850	1	1		2
Mordecai Haynes	October 15, 1850			5	5
Nathan Childs	October 15, 1850	1	1	4	6
Philip Cissel	October 15, 1850	3	3	4	10
Phillip Smallwood	October 15, 1850	1	2	3	6
Rachel Gaither	October 15, 1850	2	2		4
Rebecca Cole	October 15, 1850		1		1
Richard Nicholson	October 15, 1850			1	1
Richard Pindle	October 15, 1850		1	1	2

OWNER	DATE	MALE	FEMALE	CHILDREN	TOTAL
Samuel Cissel	October 15, 1850	3	1	1	5
Samuel Harding	October 15, 1850			1	1
William H. Hardy	October 15, 1850		1	4	5
William Iglehart	October 15, 1850			1	1
William P. Ridgely	October 15, 1850	1	2	1	4
William Simpson	October 15, 1850		2		2
Ann Jenkins	October 20, 1850		1	2	3
Ellen Harcy	October 20, 1850		2	5	7
George C. Pierce	October 20, 1850			2	2
George H. Waters	October 20, 1850	1	1	2	4
George W. Richardson	October 20, 1850			2	2
John Watkins	October 20, 1850	3	1	5	9
Mary Iglehart	October 20, 1850		1	2	3
Samuel Nichols	October 20, 1850		1	1	2
Upton Dorsey	October 20, 1850	1	1	6	8
William Hardy	October 20, 1850	2	1	1	4
Abraham Albaugh	October 21, 1850			1	1
Charles Mactavish	October 21, 1850	25	7	18	50
James Treakle	October 21, 1850	1	3	6	10
Wesley Linthicum	October 21, 1850	6	5	12	23
William W. Watkins	October 21, 1850		2	5	7
Z. Cissel	October 21, 1850			1	1
Charlotte Spurrier	October 22, 1850	2	1	4	7
Edward Bryan	October 22, 1850	2			2
Horatia Johnson	October 22, 1850		1		1
James Dill	October 22, 1850	2			2
John Holland	October 22, 1850	1	2	5	8
John Honnel	October 22, 1850	1	2		3
John L. Marace	October 22, 1850	1	1		2
John Russel	October 22, 1850			1	1
Joseph W. Tyson	October 22, 1850	2	2	1	5
Larkin Iglehart	October 22, 1850			1	1
Leonard Eatson	October 22, 1850	1	2	1	4
Margaret Iglehart	October 22, 1850	4	2	9	15
Martin H. Batson	October 22, 1850	2	2	5	9
Rachel Clark	October 22, 1850	1	1	3	5
William Cark	October 22, 1850	4	2	4	12

OWNER	DATE	MALE	FEMALE	CHILDREN	TOTAL
Albert G. Warfield	October 25, 1850	5	3	1	9
Elizabeth A. Marriott	October 25, 1850			1	1
Elizabeth B. Macheu	October 25, 1850	2	2	5	9
Joseph Snyder	October 25, 1850		2		2
Mortimer Dorsey	October 25, 1850	4	2	6	12
Perry Gaither	October 25, 1850	2	1	5	8
Philemon Dorsey	October 25, 1850		1	4	6
Rachel Warfield	October 25, 1850	2	4	11	17
Richard M. Downs	October 25, 1850		1		2
Samuel Owings	October 25, 1850	2	2	1	5
William Owings	October 25, 1850		1	3	5
Adam C. Warner	October 30, 1850		4	4	9
Basil Duvall	October 30, 1850	2	1	1	4
Edmond Warfield	October 30, 1850		1	3	4
Elizabeth H. Bapates	October 30, 1850		1	2	3
Ephrium Warfield	October 30, 1850	2	1		3
Jacob Young	October 30, 1850				1
James A. Meredith	October 30, 1850	3		3	6
James Boxley	October 30, 1850	3	4	5	12
James M. Thompson	October 30, 1850				1
John D. Warfield	October 30, 1850		1	2	4
John G. Crapster	October 30, 1850		3	7	11
Jonathan Steart	October 30, 1850				1
Nicholas B. Warfield	October 30, 1850		3	7	11
Sarah Warfield	October 30, 1850		1	4	5
William Davis	October 30, 1850		1	2	3
William P. Warfield	October 30, 1850	5	3		8
Wilson D. Warfield	October 30, 1850			1	1
Adam Warner	October 31, 1850			4	4
Allen Ser	October 31, 1850				1
Catharine Dorsey	October 31, 1850		1	1	2
Christian Close	October 31, 1850	3	1		3
David Clark	October 31, 1850		3	7	11
Eli Molesworth	October 31, 1850		1		1
Francis M. Shipley	October 31, 1850		1	2	3
Greenbury Gaither	October 31, 1850			5	6
Henry Welsh	October 31, 1850	2			2

OWNER	DATE	MALE	FEMALE	CHILDREN	TOTAL
Horatio Crawford	October 31, 1850			1	1
Ignatius Waters	October 31, 1850	1	1	5	7
James Harban	October 31, 1850			2	2
John H. Owings	October 31, 1850	3		4	7
John Ozun	October 31, 1850	1	1	1	3
Jonathan Mullings	October 31, 1850			1	1
Lloyd Linthicum	October 31, 1850	1	1	2	4
Lorenzo G. Warfield	October 31, 1850	1	1	2	4
Milton Welsh	October 31, 1850	2	2	5	9
Phebe Dorsey	October 31, 1850			1	1
Robert Mullings	October 31, 1850			1	1
Samuel Banks	October 31, 1850	6	7	16	29
Stephen B. Dorsey	October 31, 1850	1	1	3	5
Agustus Riggs	November 6, 1850		2		2
Artemias Hearn	November 6, 1850		1	3	4
Elizabeth R. Snowden	November 6, 1850			1	1
Evan Warfield	November 6, 1850			1	1
Gustavus Warfield	November 6, 1850	6	1	8	15
Humphrey Dorsey	November 6, 1850	1			1
James B. Matthews	November 6, 1850	1	3	9	13
Joshua Moore	November 6, 1850			2	2
Stephen Musgrove	November 6, 1850	1			1
Thomas Cook	November 6, 1850	4	4	6	14
Alfred C. Hearn	November 9, 1850	1	1	5	7
Basil Crapster	November 9, 1850	3	3	3	9
Benjamin Hearn	November 9, 1850	1			1
Brigold Smith	November 9, 1850		1		1
Charles C. Owings	November 9, 1850			1	1
Charles D. Warfield	November 9, 1850	7	4	9	20
Charles Ridgely	November 9, 1850	3	2	2	7
George W. Hobbs	November 9, 1850	1	2	6	9
John Whelan	November 9, 1850	1	1	2	4
Joshua H. Cross	November 9, 1850			1	1
Lewis Ridgely	November 9, 1850	1		1	2
Mahlon Sappell	November 9, 1850			1	1
Richard Hearn	November 9, 1850		1	1	2
Rosanne Morgan	November 9, 1850	1	1	1	3
Samuel Ridgely	November 9, 1850	1	1	4	6
Thomas Petticord	November 9, 1850		1		1
Tighlman Iglehart	November 9, 1850	1	1	3	5
Walter Dorsey	November 9, 1850		1	2	3
William Cushen	November 9, 1850	1		2	3
A. Warfield	November 14, 1850		1		1
Asbury Petticord	November 14, 1850		1	3	4
Caleb Dorsey	November 14, 1850	4	2	5	11
Caleb Petticord	November 14, 1850			1	1
Caleb Shipley Inn	November 14, 1850	1			1
Charles A. Hobbs	November 14, 1850	1			1
Christian Wallick	November 14, 1850		1	3	4
David Lemmon	November 14, 1850	1		4	5
Deborah Edmondson	November 14, 1850	1			1
Gerard Hobbs	November 14, 1850	1		1	2
James H. Hobbs	November 14, 1850		1		1
James Henderson	November 14, 1850	1		3	4
John C. Mercer	November 14, 1850		1		1
John Fishen	November 14, 1850		1		1
Jonathan Hopkins	November 14, 1850		1		1
Jonathan Miller	November 14, 1850	1	1	2	4
Lemuel Warfield	November 14, 1850	3	3	6	12
Nancy Lansdale	November 14, 1850			3	3
Nathan C. Hobbs	November 14, 1850		1		1
Nathan Shipley	November 14, 1850	2	1	5	8
Peregrine Hobbs	November 14, 1850		2	5	7
Rachel Leach	November 14, 1850		1		1
Robert H. Howard	November 14, 1850	1			1
Talbot G. Shipley	November 14, 1850		1	2	3
Thomas B. Hobbs	November 14, 1850			2	2
Thomas Barnis	November 14, 1850	1			1
Thomas H. Hood	November 14, 1850	1	1	2	4
Thomas Lucy Inn	November 14, 1850			1	1
William Crockett	November 14, 1850	1			1
William Petticord	November 14, 1850			1	1
Zacharia Davis	November 14, 1850	2	1	1	4
Abram England	November 18, 1850		1		1

OWNER	DATE	MALE	FEMALE	CHILDREN	TOTAL
Ann Dorsey	November 18, 1850			1	1
Artemas Riggs	November 18, 1850		1	3	4
Basil Owings	November 18, 1850		1	3	4
David Burkett	November 18, 1850			1	1
E. Hobbs	November 18, 1850			1	1
George Warfield	November 18, 1850	2	1	7	10
Joseph Lyle	November 18, 1850	1	1	4	6
Joshua Ennis	November 18, 1850			1	1
Maria McGee	November 18, 1850	1			1
Philemon D. Warfield	November 18, 1850	6	4	7	17
Robert Hood	November 18, 1850			1	1
Roderick Dorsey	November 18, 1850	2	1	3	6
Samuel Dorsey	November 18, 1850	3	1	4	8
Samuel G. Matthews	November 18, 1850		1	1	2
Samuel Spigg	November 18, 1850		1		1
William Inge	November 18, 1850			1	1
William Webb	November 18, 1850	2	1	4	7
A. Mercer	November 25, 1850			1	1
Bela Warfield	November 25, 1850		1	5	6
Benjamin Hood	November 25, 1850	2	1	3	6
Charles Hensey	November 25, 1850	1	1	7	9
Edmond Iglehart	November 25, 1850			1	1
Elizabeth Warfield	November 25, 1850			1	1
Hannah Sheets	November 25, 1850	2		2	4
Henry Hipsey	November 25, 1850	1		2	3
Henry Ridgely	November 25, 1850	1	1	1	3
James Mitchell	November 25, 1850		1		1
James Sykes	November 25, 1850	5	3	2	10
John Hood	November 25, 1850	3	2	4	9
John W. Mercen	November 25, 1850			1	1
Joshua Wright	November 25, 1850		1		1
Levi Chambers	November 25, 1850	1	1	2	4
Marcellus Warfield	November 25, 1850			1	1
Nicholas Owings	November 25, 1850	1	1	2	4
R. Warfield	November 25, 1850	1	1		2
Samuel Gaither	November 25, 1850	2	1	2	5
Upton Wade	November 25, 1850	1			1

OWNER	DATE	MALE	FEMALE	CHILDREN	TOTAL
Washington Gaither	November 25, 1850	2		4	6
Washington Peddicord	November 25, 1850		1		1
William Warfield	November 25, 1850			2	3
Andrew Mercen	December 1, 1850		3	6	10
Beal Whalen	December 1, 1850			5	6
Charles Booth	December 1, 1850			1	2
Elizabeth Mercen	December 1, 1850	2			2
Henry Forsyth	December 1, 1850	1		3	4
Howes Goldsboro	December 1, 1850		1	2	3
Isaac C. Anderson	December 1, 1850	8	3	14	25
Isaac C. Rowles	December 1, 1850	2	1	4	7
John A. Dorsey	December 1, 1850	1	1	8	10
John Adair	December 1, 1850		1		1
John Forsyth	December 1, 1850	2	1		3
Joseph Paxon	December 1, 1850	1			1
Michael Hackett	December 1, 1850			1	1
R.D. Hewitt	December 1, 1850	2	1		3
Robert Hardin	December 1, 1850	2	1	1	4
Thomas C. Herbert	December 1, 1850	2		2	4
Upton D. Welsh	December 1, 1850	2		1	4
Wesley Whalen	December 1, 1850		1		1
William H. Marriott	December 1, 1850	5		5	10
Amana D. Whalen	December 5, 1850	1		3	4
Ann D. Polton	December 5, 1850	1	1		2
Joshua Barlou	December 5, 1850			1	1
Julian Warfield	December 5, 1850	1	1	2	4
R. Hammond	December 5, 1850	2			2
Samuel Dorsey	December 5, 1850	9	3	5	17
Sarah Brown	December 5, 1850		1		1
Thomas Anderson	December 5, 1850	3	2	13	18
Vachel Harding	December 5, 1850	3	3	13	19
Amelia Shipley	December 7, 1850	1	2	1	4
Andrew Dorsey	December 7, 1850		1	4	5
Charles R. Howard	December 7, 1850	4	2	17	23
Dr. Richard G. Stockett	December 7, 1850	3	4	9	19
Mrs. Lincoln Phelps	December 7, 1850	1	1		2
Samuel Brown	December 7, 1850	3	1	10	14
Susanna Brown	December 7, 1850	1	1	3	5

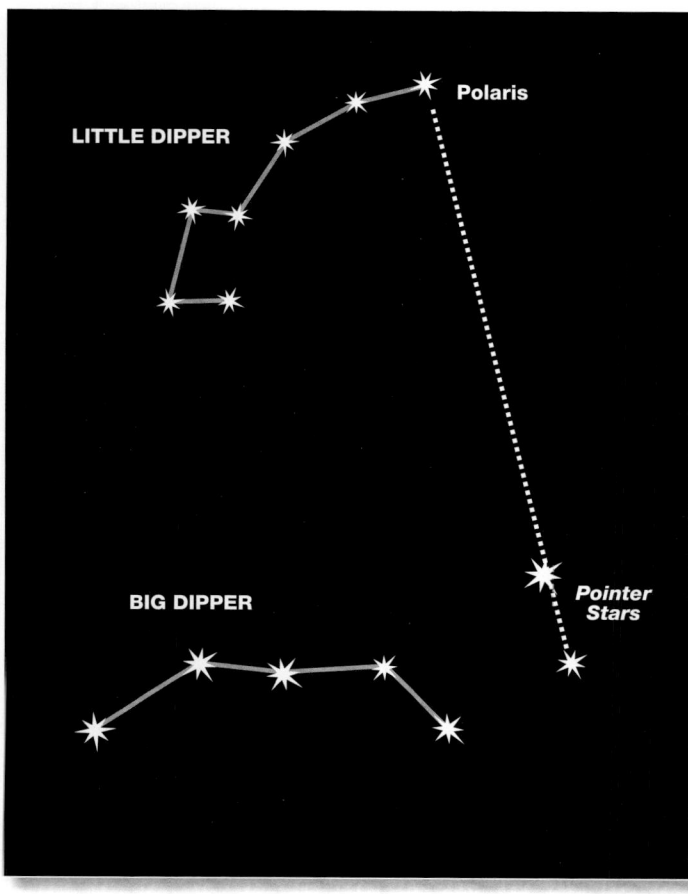

The "Drinking Gourd," or Big Dipper, points to Polaris, the North star. Using this orientation of the stars as a guide, one could travel north toward the "free states" without much other guidance.

When the sun comes up, and the first quail calls,
Follow the drinking gourd,
For the old man is a-waiting for to carry you to freedom
If you follow the drinking gourd.
  Follow...

Means of Escape

Howard County was geographically favorable to the Underground Railroad because of its landscape, waterways, and its transportation systems which provided means of escape. The county is bound on the east by the Patapsco River, and on the south and west by the Patuxent River. The Baltimore-Frederick Pike was located near the northern border of the county. The Pike was utilized for transporting goods between Frederick County and Baltimore City Seaport. The southern route lent itself to navigation on the Patuxent River and on to Baltimore and Philadelphia. All routes provided a method of transportation for fugitives attempting to enter a northern state.

Another means of escape was the Thomas Viaduct built by the B&O Railroad (Baltimore and Ohio). It is still in existence and in use by the commercial railroad system. It crossed the Patapsco River, traveling from Relay to Elkridge, then continuing on to Laurel and into Washington, D.C. Those escaping hid in culverts of the viaduct until the arrival of the train to board and hide.

Rethinking Slavery in the County

In 1776, Charles Carroll of Carrollton was sent to Philadelphia, as a delegate to the Second Continental Congress, and while there signed the Declaration of Independence. Upon his return, Carroll realized the hypocrisy in signing the Declaration of Independence and continuing to own slaves. He began to champion the abolitionist cause.

In the mid-seventeenth through the mid-eighteenth centuries, tobacco had an expanding market in the county. However, after years of planting tobacco, the soil began to deteriorate and lose its nutrients the once-fertile lands were exhausted. Wheat and hay began to replace tobacco. The Ellicott brothers had mills built for the grinding of wheat for flour and other produce. Whites provided the labor for mill work and slave labor became less valuable.

Source: Maryland Historical Trust

The Thomas Viaduct, completed in 1835 to carry the B&O Railroad across the Patapsco River, was a landmark for slaves making their way north along the train tracks.

SLAVERY IN HOWARD COUNTY 25

After Slavery in the County

In 1864, Maryland passed a law to abolish slavery in the state. The prominent families of the period maintained their properties, willing their assets to descendants over the ensuing years. These descendants became the controllers of the economic and political life of the county, and became active in state politics.

Churches served as schools, as well as for religious purposes. African American families, who were landowners, were able to maintain their land and homes, and pass their properties on to their descendants. Education became a priority for blacks as stated in a paper prepared by the Howard County Branch of the NAACP in 1986 and continues to be a priority for black families. It is an avenue that elevates many blacks to middle and upper class status.

*Locust United Methodist Church
Simpsonville, Maryland*

The First Established Churches In Howard County from 1843 – 1875:

1843	First Baptist Church of Elkridge	Elkridge, Maryland
1859	Asbury United Methodist Church	Jessup, Maryland
1860	Gaines African Methodist Episcopal Church (formerly Providence)	Elkridge, Maryland
1860	Hopkins United Methodist Church	Highland, Maryland
1860	St. Stephens AME Church	Elkridge, Maryland
1860	St. Luke's AME Church	Ellicott City, Maryland
1869	Locust United Methodist Church	Simpsonville, Maryland
1870	Mt. Gregory United Methodist Church	Cooksville, Maryland
1870	Mt. Zion United Methodist Church	Ellicott City, Maryland
1875	West Liberty United Methodist (formerly Woodford United Methodist)	Marriottsville, Maryland

The County in the Year 2000

Howard County is a successful blend of the old and the new. It is both urban and rural. It is home to over 252,000 people, a setting where one of the most modern cities in the world sits side by side with a city older than America. Ellicott City celebrated its bicentennial in 1972, four years before the United States, while Columbia the metropolitan center was carved out of the rolling Howard County farmland only thirty-four years ago.[2]

Harriet Tubman stood out as the icon of the Underground Railroad and was called the "Moses of her people." She was born into slavery about 1820 on the Edward Brodas plantation in Dorchester County Maryland. Born to Harriet Green and Benjamin Ross, Harriet was named Araminta Ross, but was later called Harriet after her mother. In danger of being sold away from her husband, John Tubman, a free Black and her extended family, she escaped alone in 1848 to Philadelphia. She returned to Maryland's Eastern Shore area about 20 times and led more than 300 runaways to freedom. During the Civil War, she returned to the United States from Saint Catharines, Canada, where she had settled, and served in the Union Army as a nurse, spy, and scout. Tubman died in 1913 at age 93.

> "I looked at my hands to see if I was the same person now I was free.
>
> There was such a glory over everything, …
>
> I felt like I was in heaven."
>
> – Harriet Tubman
> Nurse, Spy, Scout and Liberator

References

1. Voris, Helen, P., *Elkridge: Where It All Began*, Elkridge, Maryland 2000. Pg. 13

2. "Howard County Area History," (www.howardcountymd.com/historyhcr). Pg. 1

PART I
Section C

Early Columbia and Columbia, a Planned Community

Historical Chronology of Columbia

1963	Rouse Company announced the purchase of 21 square miles for a new city
1967	Opening of Columbia, Maryland, a planned community
2000	91,140 total population of Columbia

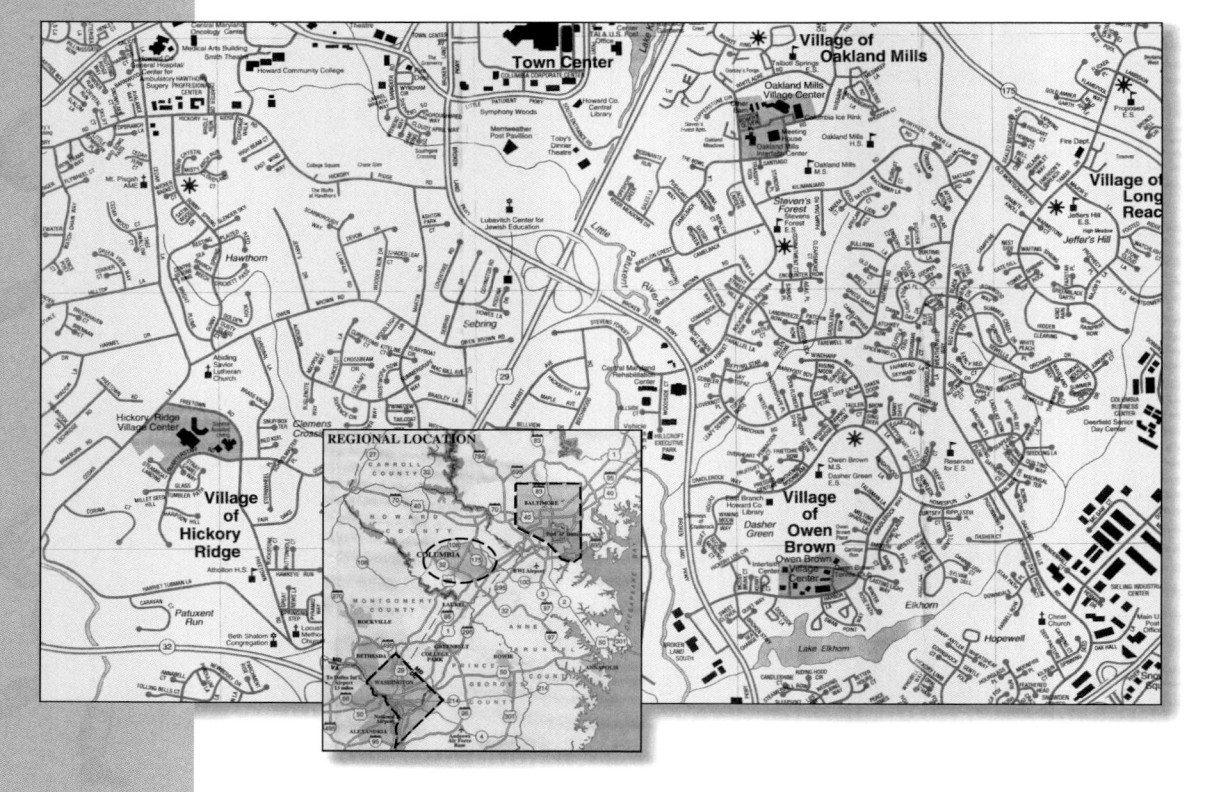

Early Columbia

The original Columbia was the meeting point of roads leading from Annapolis, Laurel and Sandy Spring to Ellicott City. This meeting point developed into a small village. It appeared after the American Revolution and obtained the name of Columbia from a Post Office that was in need of a name for its location. In an earlier period, Algonquin Indians lived, fished and hunted on these lands.

Means of Escape From the Area Now Known as Columbia

The area on which Columbia is now located provided means of escape to those held in bondage. Harriet Tubman was able to pass through Freetown, where the African American population was free. A cave at Cedar Lane has been verified as an UGR hiding place. Hogheads, the very large barrels in which tobacco was stored, offered a means of hiding. Creeks and cemeteries also provided safe havens for runaways.

Columbia, Maryland Established – A Planned Community

In the early sixties, the visionary James Rouse, a small town boy turned real estate developer, eyed the large tracts of farmland in Howard County with a dream of building a city. Rouse dreamed of not just an ordinary city, but a planned community. Rouse knew that Howard County was the geographic bridge of farmland between Baltimore and Washington, DC, which perfectly suited his vision. With $23 million promised by interested parties, he obtained the services of attorneys to buy the required land. Connecticut General Life Insurance was the primary investor of the $23 million.

James Rouse called together a group of educators, social scientists and urban planners to confer about the new project. With their input, the foundation of the new town was laid: a democratic, egalitarian housing community of diverse racial and religious backgrounds. The city would be comprised of several villages. Each village would cover specific geographic boundaries, and would include schools, shops, markets, recreation areas and a common public patio or square. The initial plans included future plans for a major shopping mall, theaters, hotels, recreational and religious facilities as well as facilities for boating.

In 1967, the city of Columbia opened in Howard County. "James Rouse decided to call his new city "Columbia", because it had a "hallelujah sound to it."[1] Since its origin in 1967, Columbia has continued to dedicate itself to maintaining its original concept. The population of Columbia in December 2000 was 90,000.[2]

Rochester, August 29, 1868

Dear Harriet:

I am glad to know that the story of your wonderful life has been written by a kindly lady, and that the same is soon to be published. You ask what you do not need when you call upon me for a word of commendation. I need such words from you far more than you can need them from me, especially where your superior labors and devotion to the cause of the lately enslaved of our land are known as I know them. The differences between us are very marked. Most that I have done and suffered in the service of our cause has been in public; and I have received much encouragement at every step of the way. I have wrought in the day—you in the night. I have had the applause of the crowd and the satisfaction that comes of being approved by the multitude, while the most that you have done has been witnessed by a few trembling, scarred, and footsore bondmen and women, whom you have led out of the house of bondage, and whose heartfelt, "God bless you," has been your only reward.

The midnight sky and the silent stars have been the witnesses of your devotion to freedom and of your heroism — excepting John Brown — of sacred memory — I know of no one who has willingly encountered more perils and hardships to serve our enslaved people than you have.

Much that you have done would seem improbable to those who do not know you as I know you. It is to me a great pleasure and a great privilege to bear testimony to your character and your work, and to say to those to whom you may come, that I regard you in every way truthful and trustworthy.[3]

Your friend,

Frederick Douglass

Conclusion

Looking at what is now Columbia, Maryland, it is hard to believe its early history of slavery and the Underground Railroad. Rouse's vision of a new planned community, where the descendants of slaves and descendants of slave owners could live together in harmony appears successful. However, any authentic history of Columbia, Maryland must include its early history of slaves' help in developing the area and their heroic escape to freedom.

> "Presumption should never make us neglect that which appears easy to us, nor despair make us lose courage at the sight of difficulties."
>
> – Benjamin Banneker, 1794

REFERENCES

1. Hobby, David and Susan Thornton, *Columbia, A Celebration*, Columbia, Maryland: Perry Publishing, 1995, Pg. 20

2. Howard County Research and Development Corporation, *Columbia, Maryland Status Report*, Columbia, Maryland: Rouse Company, December, 2000

3. Foner, Philip S., Editor, *The Life and Writings of Frederick Douglass*, International Publishers, NY, 1954, Four Volumes, Vol. 4, Pg. 211–212

PART II

Underground Railroad Stops in Howard County

Historical Chronology of the Underground Railroad

1830	The term Underground Railroad was first used
1840	Underground Railroad first appeared in print
1830 – 1865	The peak period of the Underground Railroad

"I would fight for my liberty as long as my strength lasted, and if the time came for me to go, the Lord would let them take me."

– Harriet Tubman

Harriet Tubman by Huey Lee-Smith
Photographed by Laurence Hurst
Collection: Banneker-Douglass Museum, Annapolis, Maryland

When the Underground Railroad Started

Harriet Tubman and thousands of other slaves risked their lives for liberty by escaping on the Underground Railroad (UGR). Tubman was a major conductor on the UGR. *Conductors* led thousands of slaves to escape from bondage. Fugitive slaves were called *Passengers*. Houses where fugitive slaves hid were called *Stations*. *Station Masters* allowed fugitive slaves to hide in their homes or other cover-ups such as wagons. Station Masters assisted Tubman and other conductors by hiding, housing and feeding slave fugitives traveling on the UGR. Secret codes and landmarks were used for directions from one UGR stop to another.

The term, "Underground Railroad," was used to describe a method that provided passage to enslaved fugitives attempting to escape from bondage in the southern states. The UGR was not a neatly defined system of railroad tracks, rather it was a loose association of people, places and landmarks. Freed blacks, Quakers and other white abolitionists who opposed slavery, provided runaways with food, clothing, directions, and places to hide. "Some southern slaves also helped fugitives slaves to escape." The movement allowed over 100,000 slaves to escape from bondage during the mid-1800's.

"The term, "Underground Railroad," was first used in 1830."[2] It first appeared in print in 1840. The peak period of the UGR was between 1830–1865. In 1865, during the peak of the UGR, James L. Bradley wrote the following:

From the time I was fourteen years old, I used to think a great deal about freedom. It was my heart's desire; I could not keep it off my mind. Many a sleepless night I have spent in tears, because I was called a slave. My heart ached to feel within me the life of liberty

– James Bradley

When Bradley wrote of his quest for freedom, the Underground Railroad movement was well established. It was a movement that could aid young Bradley in his heart's desire to feel within him the joy of life and liberty.

Codes of the Underground Railroad

There was a special language, signals, secret words, and secret messages that only those escaping and those who helped them understood.

Slave owners were pleased when their slaves took up crafts such as quilt making. Unbeknownst to the owners, the quilts contained secret codes. Quilts were left out to dry with the codes exposed to signal an upcoming escape or give directions to escapees who were passing through.

In order to become involved in this position, station masters had to memorize all of the secret words, signals, and secret messages.[3]

A Narrative of Joe Nick
AN ACTUAL ACCOUNT
Ellicott City, Maryland

Joe Nick, referred to as "Old Nick" was "owned" by Reuben Rogers, a lawyer and farmer in Howard County. His farm was two and one-half miles outside of Ellicott City on Main Street, extended. He could read and write, and was a skilled mechanic and wheelwright.

In 1864 or 1865 Joe Nick ran away, possibly to join the Union Army. He drove a pair of horses hitched to a covered wagon to Ellicott City. The horses were found but not Joe Nick. Rogers offered a reward of $100.00.

"Old Joe had left Ellicott City on a freight train going west, which he hopped when it was stalled on the Baltimore and Ohio Railroad a short distance from the railroad station at Ellicott City. Old Joe could not leave on the passenger train, as no Negro would be allowed on the trains unless he had a pass signed by his master or by a free Negro and had his papers."

"In June of 1865 Old Nick returned to Ellicott City dressed in a uniform of blue, showing that he had joined the Federal Army. Mr. Reuben Rogers upon seeing him had him arrested, charging him with being a fugitive slave. He was confined in jail there and held until the U.S. Marshal of Baltimore released him. The U.S. Marshal then arrested Rogers and brought him to Baltimore City where he was reprimanded by the Federal Judge."[4]

SPECIAL DEFINITIONS

ESCAPING PERSON	A passenger
STATION MASTERS	Those who sheltered and provided food and clothing
CONDUCTORS	Those who led the escaping fugitives from one secret hiding place to another (such as barns, attics, and abandoned houses)
STATIONS OR DEPOTS	Where the escapees stopped for food and clothing
FUEL	Food and clothing

SIGNALS

CLOSED FIST	It is safe to travel
OPEN HAND	Danger!
FORWARD (MOTION)	Send fugitive on to next station
SINGLE CANDLE	Path is clear
TWO CANDLES	Danger!

QUILT CODES

MONKEY WRENCH DESIGN	Gather all the tools you might need on your journey
WAGON WHEEL DESIGN	You will be traveling by wagon
TUMBLING BOXES DESIGN	Now is the time to leave

Underground Railroad in Howard County

It has been established that an extensive Underground Railroad movement existed in Howard County. The county's geographic assets provided many means of escape such as rivers, forests, caves, and culverts. The location of the county, just south of Pennsylvania, played a major role. Historians claim that the most heavily traveled routes of the UGR ran through Ohio, Indiana and Western Pennsylvania.[5] The state of Pennsylvania joins Maryland to the north, while Indiana and Ohio lie northwest of Maryland. The fact that freed blacks, Quakers and other white abolitionists lived in the county was significant. All these factors played an important part in the success of the UGR.

It is reported that Harriet Tubman led fugitives escaping bondage through what is now known as the Simpsonville and the Elkridge areas of Howard County. While the exact route of the complete Underground Railroad in Howard County cannot be drawn up, our research uncovered the information presented here on several sites used in the Underground Railroad in the Simpsonville and Elkridge areas in Howard County, Maryland.

Because the UGR was both secretive and dangerous, few records were written about its whereabouts. Therefore, little or no documentation remains about the UGR either nationally or locally. In our research of the Underground Railroad sites in Howard County, we relied on secondary sources such as those from the Maryland Historical Society, Maryland Historical Trust, local historians, and oral interviews of direct descendants of slaves in the county. (*See references.*)

UNDERGROUND RAILROAD STOPS IN HOWARD COUNTY 35

Source: Baptist Hymnal by Willa A. Townsend

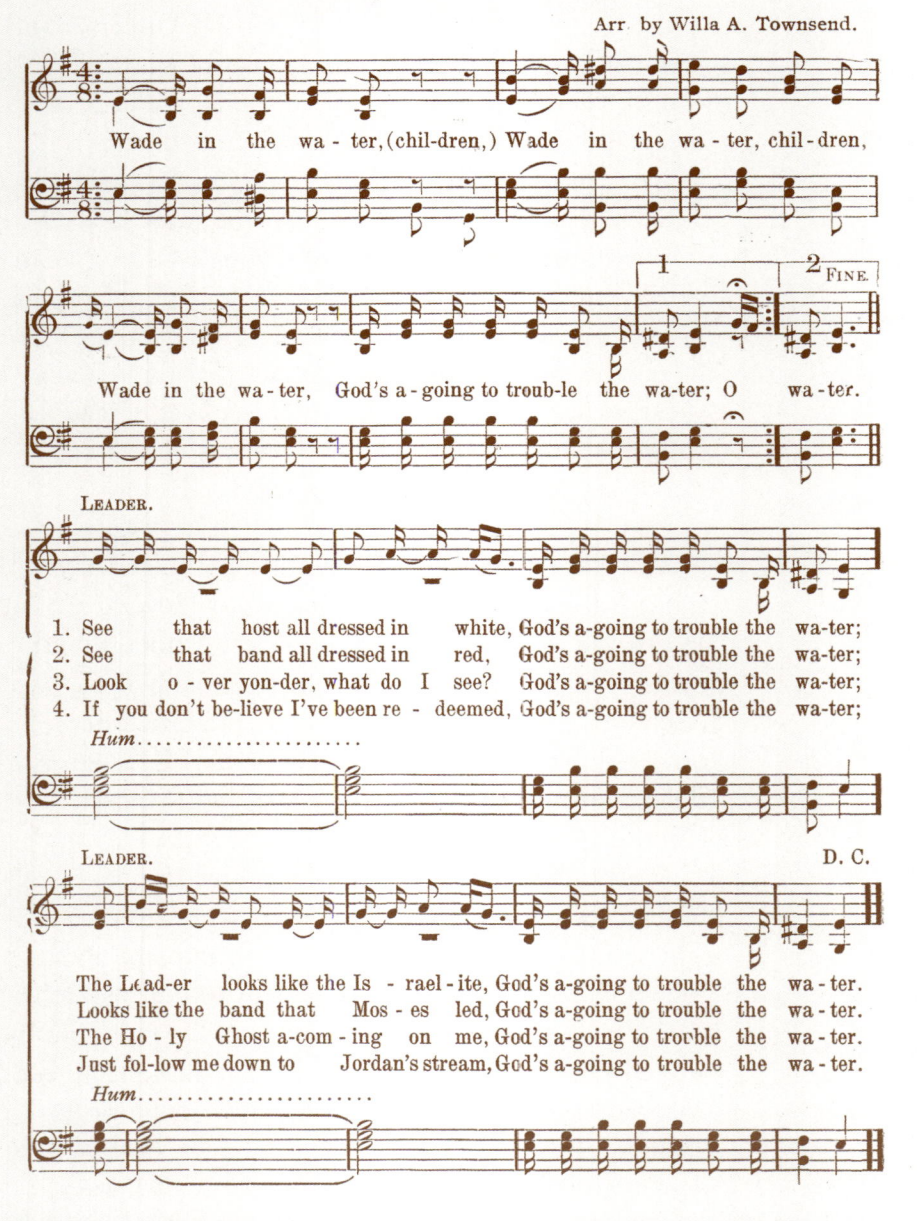

Freetown ~ Simpsonville, Maryland

If you drive south on Route 29 in Howard County, Maryland and turn off at the Seneca Drive/Martin's Road exit you are right in the middle of what used to be an old freed slave settlement called "Freetown." It is reported that in 1845, a slave owner, Nicholas Worthington upon his death, freed his 17 slaves and gave them 150 acres of land being part of the tract land called "Athol Enlarged" which became known as "Freetown". Fifteen slaves each received a sum of between $30 to $40 dollars in cash. One received $100 and another received $500. These were large sums in 1845.

Old "Freetown" was originally bound by Cedar Lane down to Route 216, continued up around Howard Community College and over to the Owen Brown area. Today all that is left of the old "Freetown" is Freetown Road, the Harriet Tubman Lane portion of Guilford Road, and Locust United Methodist Church and Cemetery.

Oral history says that Harriet Tubman led hundreds of slaves to freedom by the Underground Railroad which partially ran through Freetown in Howard County.

The following sites are where slaves were led to hide from the slave raiders in Freetown:

$75 REWARD

RANAWAY from the subscriber, on the night of the 8th inst., a NEGRO GIRL, calls herself HARRIET GREEN, 16 or 17 years of age, a very bright mulatto, at a little distance would be taken for white; hair straight and black, being a little sun burnt, rather low set, not being over four feet ten inches high. Down look when spoken to and large grey eyes. Took with her one blue plaid frock (domestic), one blue calico dress, straw bonnet, with flair in front trimmed with white ribbon. I will pay the above reward if returned to me.

SIMPSONVILLE, MARYLAND

PERSONAL

$C REWARD — RANAWAY on the 21st March, a colored boy, named BENJAMIN COOK, about 20 years old, an apprentice to the Harness Making business. All persons are cautioned against harboring him, as the law will be enforced against them. The above reward, but no charges, will be paid to any person returning him to me.

James BRICARD,
Ellicott's Mills

INDIAN CAVE ~ SIMPSONVILLE, MARYLAND

At the bottom of a hill on the north bank of Route 32 and Cedar Lane in old Freetown sits a cavity in a large boulder known as Indian Cave. The cave is located in a very secluded area just across the street from the Middle Patuxent Creek. Legend has it that before the Civil War, a story circulated about nine runaway slaves who hid themselves in a cave near Route 32 and Cedar Lane. Either intentionally or inadvertently, they avoided destroying a spiderweb at the mouth of the cave. When bounty hunters rode by, they shouted that the runaways couldn't be in the cave because the spider web wasn't disturbed." [6]

Courtesy: Larry Crouse

UNDERGROUND RAILROAD STOPS IN HOWARD COUNTY 37

QUAKER SAFE HOUSE
SIMPSONVILLE, MARYLAND

The Quaker Safe House is at the end of Guilford Road known as Harriet Tubman Lane. The original Quaker House burned and was replaced circa 1890. Harriet Tubman was known to have stayed at Quaker Safe Houses.

LOCUST UNITED METHODIST CHURCH CEMETERY
SIMPSONVILLE, MARYLAND

If you drive south on Route 29 in Howard County and exit at Seneca Drive/Martin's Road, make a right at the top of the ramp; then, a left onto Martin's Road and proceed for about a mile; you will see Locust United Methodist Church and the Cemetery just beyond the grove to the right. Tubman and fleeing slaves are said to have hid at this grave site.[7]

$300 REWARD

RANAWAY from the subscriber—living on Elk Ridge, in Howard District of Anne Arundel county, Md., on Sunday, the 22d instant, negro REMUS KELLY. Remus is a dark copper colored mulatto with a bluff, full face, heavy eye-brows, and rather a bushy head. He is about 19 years old, 5 feet 9 or 10 inches high, of a stout athletic frame, stammers when spoken to, and stoops a little in the shoulders. Had on when he left home a blue frock coat, white pantaloons, white cotton shirt, hat and boots. Remus is a blacksmith and served a time with Harry Calhoun, a free negro near Ellicott's Mills. I will give a reward of ONE HUNDRED DOLLARS for his apprehension, if he is secured in jail so that I get him again.
W. W. WATKINS
Carlsville Post Office,
Howard District, A.A. County, Maryland

I am also authorized to offer a REWARD of ONE HUNDRED DOLLARS for NEGRO GEORGE who absconded from Upton Dorsey, of Howard District. George is a stout black fellow, nearly 6 feet high; wears his hair sometimes plaited, and when not plaited, it presents a very bushy appearance at the sides of his head. George made his escape from Howard District jail about a month ago, but was seen in the neighborhood on Saturday last, the 21st inst., and is supposed to have made off in company with Remus.
W. W. WATKINS
on the 22d instant.

I have every reason to believe also, that a REWARD of ONE HUNDRED DOLLARS will be offered in a few days for NEGRO ISAAC, who absconded at the same time from the same neighborhood, from Mr. Samuel Waters. Mr. Waters is absent from home at this time, but so soon as he returns, I am sure will offer the above reward. Isaac is a black boy, about 23 or 24 years old, about 5 feet 8 or 9 inches high, rather a slender frame; clothing, and other marks not known. He is supposed to have gone off with the other two.
W. W. WATKINS

MIDDLE PATUXENT CREEK ~ SIMPSONVILLE, MARYLAND

At the bottom of the hill, on the south side of Route 32 and Cedar Lane in old Freetown, sits the Middle Patuxent Creek. Next to the bank of this Creek, Tubman and others hid from the Slave Raiders.

Courtesy: Larry Crouse

DEEP RUN — ELKRIDGE, MARYLAND

Deep Run is a long isolated stream in Elkridge. Oral history places Deep Run as a site on the Underground Railroad in Elkridge. Reverend Roland Howard remembers scrambling down the steep western bank of Deep Run. Reverend Howard is a direct descendant of Phil Gardener who was a slave. He said his maternal grandfather, Phil Gardener, told stories about Harriet Tubman winding her way along the Deep Run and stopping there so fugitives could hide below the steep banks and sleep in caves formed by the boulders. Mr. Gardener was a slave who lived on the south side of Route 1 near Jessup where the detention center is now located. He told stories about the time Harriet Tubman stopped at the cabin for food and to get cool fresh water from the spring. He said that, "She would rest here, then they would go on to Freetown Road."[8] All the blacks on Freetown Road had been set free according to Reverend Howard.

Courtesy: Larry Crouse

FIRST BAPTIST CHURCH OF ELKRIDGE
ELKRIDGE, MARYLAND

The deed to the Trustee is dated 1843. In the earliest days of the county, in the mid-to-late 19th century, churches served not only as places of worship but as schools and community centers. Churches also served as stations on the Underground Railroad. The First Baptist Church of Elkridge was said to be used as a hiding place for runaway slaves on the UGR. The church was damaged by fire in the 1960's. The present church is situated on the same site as the original church on Paradise Avenue.

PERSONAL

$200 REWARD—RANAWAY from the subscriber residing on Elkridge, Howard District, Anne Arundel County, on the 29th inst. Two of his slaves (brothers) the elder named **GEORGE**, about 5 feet 11 inches; aged 25 years. He took a variety of clothing; very pleasant when spoken to; not very black. The younger named **HENRY**, about 5 feet 6 inches high, aged 22 years; very black; has remarkable white teeth; broad across the shoulders and stout made; has long arms; he likewise had a variety of clothing, among which is recollected a blue coat, with black velvet cape and cuffs, and striped gingham summer coat. It is supposed they are in company with two others; one of Dr. Allen Thomas', and one of N. Worthington's of the same neighborhood. Dr. Thomas' is a tall slim black fellow, about 6 feet high, and stammers. I am authorized to say he will give $100 for his, if taken and secured so he gets him again; I will give the above reward if mine are taken and secured so that I get them, or $100 for either. SAM'L BROWN, Jr., Near Ellicott's Mills

---

UNDERGROUND RAILROAD STOPS IN HOWARD COUNTY

HOWARD'S HOMEPLACE FOR FREE SLAVES ~
ELKRIDGE, MARYLAND

The Howard's "Homeplace" for Free Slaves was a log cabin. It was situated southwest of Meadowridge Road, Maryland, Route 103, (Homeplace Lane as of August 25, 1995) in the city of Elkridge. Oral history claims "Homeplace" was a rest stop for Harriet Tubman where she safely obtained water and food. It is the history of the Howard family ancestor, William Henry Howard, slave of John Eager Howard.[9] Three generations of Howards lived in this log cabin that once stood on a tract of land called "Grecian Liege." This tract of land and former log cabin were adjacent to Deep Run and used as an Underground Railroad stop.

Twenty Shillings REWARD

ELKRIDGE—RANAWAY from Elk Ridge Furnace on Friday the 13 of July, a Negro man named TOM, he is about 30 years of age, 5 feet 9 or 10 inches high, has a remarkable large scar proceeding from each of his temples down his cheeks, a well made fellow, looks a little sullen and talks pretty good English and a little French. He carried with him an old dark coloured monmouth cap (and is supposed soon after to have stole a pretty good hat and a white cap, they being missing much about that time), a good osnabrigs shirt, cotton jacket and breeches, hempen roll trowsers, and old shoes. He was formerly accustomed to go by water and probably may attempt to escape that way. He formerly belonged to Mr. Thomas Ringgold, New-Town upon Chester River, to Capt. Michael Earle, near Frederick-Town upon Sassafras River but last of all to Mr. Henry Pearce at Herring Run in Cecil County. Whoever takes up the said Runaway and brings him to the subscriber, at the Elk Ridge Furnace shall have Twenty Shillings Reward besides what the law allows…"

$100 REWARD

ELKRIDGE—RANAWAY from the subscribers farm on Elk Ridge on Saturday night the 2n instant, a negro man named HANSON, who calls himself Hanson Marshall. He is about 5 foot 6 inches high, 38-40 years old, the front of his head bald; a stout well set fellow. He is a plantation servant and a good hand with a scythe, either in grain or grass. His clothes are of strong country-made cloth, coarse shoes, and wool hat. His Sunday dress consists of a staff coat, grey pantaloons and a silk waistcoat; but as he has money it is probable he will change his clothes. He also took with him two pair oznaburg trowsers and shirt, nearly new. He has been ruptured and wears a truss. The above award will be paid on having said servant lodged in any jail in Maryland, so that I get him again.

RICHARD DORSEY

25 June 1827 Baltimore, Md.

42   SEEKING FREEDOM

THOMAS VIADUCT — ELKRIDGE, MARYLAND

The Thomas Viaduct was built in 1835. "It was named after Phillip Thomas, President of the B&O," (Baltimore & Ohio Railroad System).[10] When the B&O began using the viaduct on its journeys north, those escaping slavery hid in culverts of the viaduct until the arrival of the train to board and hide.

Courtesy: Paulina C. Moss

ONE HUNDRED DOLLARS REWARD.
RANAWAY from the subscriber, residing near Elkridge Landing, on Friday, the 1st of July, a Negro Boy, who calls himself BILL MEYER. He is 19 years old, 5 feet 5 inches high, complexion very black; has a scar on his nose and one on his cheek; has a pleasant smiling countenance when spoken to. He absconded in female apparel, consisting of a mousline de laine frock, a stomacher a black bonnet trimmed with crepe, black cotton stockings and morocco shoes. The above reward will be given on delivery of the said negro to the subscriber, or if lodged in jail, so that I get him again.
JAMES CLARK
Near Elkridge Landing, A.A. Co. Md.

ONE HUNDRED DOLLARS REWARD.
RANAWAY from near Elkridge Landing, Howard District, Maryland, on Wednesday, the 11th instant; my Negro Man, NED, who calls himself Ned Toogood. He is about 23 years of age, very black, about 5 feet 6 or 7 inches high, good-looking, with considerable wool on his head—carries himself very very good and speaks quick. Whoever takes up said Negro and secures him in jail so that I get him again, shall receive, if taken in the State $50, or, out of the State, the above reward. I understand he went off with Mrs. Bradford's man, living near the above place.
JNO. H. BROWN
near Millersville A.A. Co., Md.

RANAWAY FROM THE SUBSCRIBER
on the 7th inst a bright Mulatto GIRL about 12 years of age, named Charlotte Fisher, bound to the subscriber for a term of years. She is supposed to be in Baltimore. A liberal reward will be given for her apprehension so that I get her again.
N.M. DYSON
near Elk Ridge Landing,
Anne Arundel County

Annapolis, Maryland Gazette
August 2, 1759

Possible Underground Railroad Stops in Howard County

Source: Maryland Historical Trust

OAKLAND MANOR ~ COLUMBIA, MARYLAND

"One ironic and highly contradictory legend persists: namely that Oakland Manor served as a stop on the Underground Railroad for runaway slaves. This allegation has appeared in a number of accounts of the history of Oakland Manor despite the many known sacrifices made by the Gaithers on behalf of the Confederacy."[11] Confederate troops also are reported to have used the facilities.

44   SEEKING FREEDOM

RED HOUSE TAVERN (LISBON REGION)
COOKSVILLE, MARYLAND

The Red House Tavern, an 18th century country inn, overlooks Route 97 and borders an abandoned stretch of Old Frederick Road. The tavern served as the midway stopping point between Baltimore and Frederick for travelers. George Washington is reputed to have spent a night here. Oral history reports fugitives escaping from slavery hid in stagecoaches that stopped at the tavern. Some were concealed, others were disguised as servants to travelers sympathetic to the plight of the enslaved.

Source: Maryland Historical Trust

ROBERTS INN — COOKSVILLE, MARYLAND

This old inn is located approximately 1/8 mile from the intersection of Route 97 North at Route 144, Frederick Road, the "National Pike" from Baltimore to Frederick. It is located on the north side of the old pike and sits back from the road. General Lafayette stopped here on his historic tour of Maryland. Oral history reports that fugitive slaves hid outside in Conestoga Wagons which carried gentry men to Roberts Inn.

A Pastoral Visit by artist Richard N. Brooke

WANTED TO HIRE

A COLORED WOMAN, to cook, Wash and Iron, for a small family. Also a BOY, from 14 to 16 years of age, to have charge of a horse. Slaves would be preferred. To good servants a permanent place and liberal wages will be given.

Apply to Dr. H.P. WORTHINGTON
Near Elkridge Landing

Howard Gazette and General Advertiser
Ellicotts Mills, Maryland
Vol. II No. 36 Saturday, September 28, 1850

Source: Library of Congress

RUTH DAGGETT HOUSE OF HOODS MILLS ROAD — COOKSVILLE, MARYLAND

Homes of freed blacks were often used to harbor fugitive slaves. One such freedman was William Henry Smith who owned the Ruth Daggett House of Hoods Mills Road in Cooksville from 1855–1863. It is quite possible that fugitive slaves stayed at this freed black's house.

CLAREMONT
ELKRIDGE, MARYLAND

Claremont is located just off Lawyers Hill Road in Elkridge, Maryland. Claremont was purchased in 1857 by Dr. James Hall, an antislavery advocate, and the first president of the Maryland Colony of the American Colonization Society, located on the west coast of Africa. "There have been rumors that Dr. Hall's home, "Claremont," was a stop on the UGR. It is impossible to make certain of this, but the property has a room in the basement at the base of four chimneys which is thought to have been the hiding place for those waiting to move to the next stop."[12]

Source: Maryland Historical Trust

UNDERGROUND RAILROAD STOPS IN HOWARD COUNTY 47

Source: Maryland Historical Trust

ELKRIDGE FURNACE COMPLEX
ELKRIDGE, MARYLAND

This iron furnace operated from the 18th century into the 1860's. During its dominant period, the complex consisted of a large Federal/Greek Revival house, a frame dwelling, a company store and a dormitory for furnace workers. Slaves were housed in four 14 feet by 16 feet plank out buildings; two still remain and two were lost to floods. "The Patapsco River, then 14 feet deep, flowed directly behind the complex, just deep enough for boats to land and enter the complex, then moved north to Elkridge, and could easily have allowed for hiding places for fugitive slaves." [13]

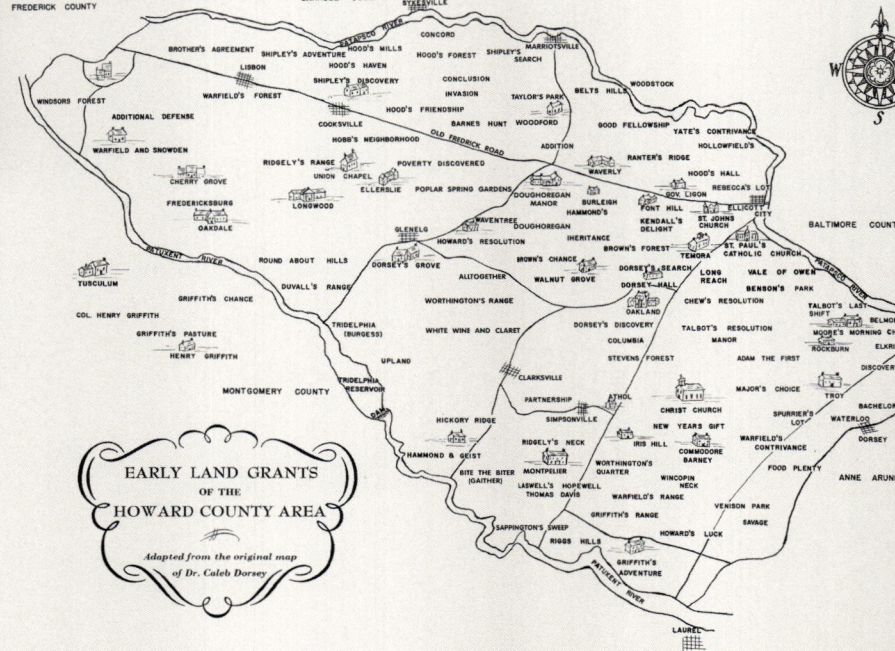

SARAH JANE DORSEY'S DEED:

...Whereas the said Sarah Hood desires to manifest her regard for Sarah Jane Dorsey, colored, late her slave for the unwavering fidelity and general good work as a servant and for that purpose has purchased from the above named J. Eugene Buck and paid him for the following described lot of land which she designs as a gift to the said Sarah Jane Dorsey. Now therefore... J. Eugene Buck, et al. grant unto the said Sarah Jane Dorsey and her children in fee simple all that parcel of land lying in Howard County, aforesaid, on the west side of the Washington Road, called "Poverty Discovered" which is contained within the following metes and bounds...

SARAH JANE DORSEY'S CABIN — COOKSVILLE, MARYLAND

On the west side of Route 97, about one-half mile south of its interchange with Route 144, sits the Sarah Jane Dorsey Log Cabin. In 1860, Thomas Hood freed his slave, Sarah Jane Dorsey (nee Powell), and gave her this cabin, her birthplace. This picturesque cabin remains one of the best preserved of the county's distinctive heirlooms. It is still occupied by descendants of Sarah Jane Dorsey.[14] While history does not record this as being a stop on the UGR, it is noteworthy that Sarah Jane Dorsey's Cabin belonged to a freed black. History records that free black homes were used in the UGR.

$300 REWARD

RANAWAY from the subscriber, near Ellicott's Mills, Howard County, Md., on Saturday inst. The 1st day of September. Negro Man, CHARLES, about five feet eight or nine inches high, dark brown complexion and thick lips. He was dressed in snuff-colored pants, thick black frock coat and light cap. He took with him a bundle containing a white shirt, white pants, and a glazed rim hat with dark brown cloth top. When spoken to he answers in a coarse, gruff voice. I will give THREE HUNDRED DOLLARS REWARD for his apprehension, if lodged in any jail in this State so that I can get him without further expense.

D.D.T. THOMPSON
Agent for owner, Ellicott's Mills, Md.

SUN–9 September 1860

STANTON LOG CABIN
ELLICOTT CITY, MARYLAND

This log cabin is believed to have been built around 1780 according to the estimates of local historians and probably served originally as a settler's hut. In 1870, this log structure provided the earliest meeting place for the organizers of the Saint Luke A.M.E. Church, now located on Main Street. The location for Saint Luke A.M.E. Church changed in 1878, to another building on the opposite side of the stream. In 1890 they moved to a new building on Main Street. It celebrated its 100th anniversary in September, 1970.

NEGRO COMMITTED

WHEREAS a Negro Man named Richard Tyler was committed to Howard District Jail on the 19th September, 1850, charged with being a Runaway. The said Negro is a dark mulatto, 23 or 24 years of age, stout and well built. He had on dark pantaloons, an old black summer cloth frock coat, and he says he is free, and that his friends live in Baltimore. This is to give notice, that if the said negro is not claimed as a Runaway within sixty days, he will be liberated according to law.

CHARLES G. HASLUP
Sh'ff of Howard District
Sept. 28, 1850

50 SEEKING FREEDOM

References

1. "The African American Journey: Underground Railroad," www.worldbook.com/fun/aajourney/html/ah040.html, Pg. 1

2. www.worldbook.com/fun/aajourney, Pg. 1

3. Blockson, Charles L., *Hippocrene Guide to the Underground Railroad*, Metcalf, Doris Hunter, African Americans, Good Apples, Inc., Parsippapy, NJ, 07054, p. 58. Reynold, Patrick M., Flashbacks, Phila.,PA.

4. Slave Narratives – A Folk History of Slavery in the U.S. from Interviews with former slaves, Kansas, Kentucky and Maryland Narratives. (Vol. 15)

5. www.worldbook.com/fun/aajourney/, Pg. 1

6. Cornelison, Alice, Silas E. Craft, Sr. and Lillie, *History of Blacks in Howard County, Maryland*, Maryland: NAACP, 1986, Pg. 6

7. Maryland Historic Sites Inventory, Survey No. HO-69, Maryland Historical Trust

8. [Interview], Beulah Buckner, 1996

9. Maryland Historic Sites Inventory, Survey No. HO-639

10. Voris, Helen P., *Elkridge: Where It All Began*, Elkridge, Maryland: Helen P. Voris, 2000, Pg. 19

11. Ibid., Pg. 36

12. Ibid., Pg. 36

13. Holland, Celia M., *Old Homes and Families in Howard County*, Maryland: privately printed, 1987, Pg. 363

14. Ibid., Pg. 239

PART III

Plantation Houses in Howard County

*"How unjust it is,
that they
who have but little
should be
always
adding something
to the wealth of the rich!"*

– Terrance (Publius Terentius Afer)

In 1851, Judge Thomas Beale Dorsey, a delegate, presented the petition of James Sykes and others asking that the Howard district in Anne Arundel County be established as a new county to be known as Howard County. By the mid-seventeenth century the institution of slavery was well established in Howard County, and so was the plantation system. Plantations were large pieces of land on which tobacco and wheat were grown in the county. Slaves were used to work the fields and grow the crops. Tobacco was the initial economy crop and later, wheat and corn.

Situated on plantations were large mansions which housed the slave owners and their families, while slaves lived in much smaller quarters. Several plantations were situated in what is now Howard County. Many of the mansions and slave quarters remain in the county as both historic landmarks and as a testimony that slavery existed here. The following are some pictorial sites of the plantation houses in Howard County.

These plantation houses are not accessible to the public

PLANTATION HOUSES IN HOWARD COUNTY 53

CLARKSVILLE

In 1790 three brothers, David, John, and James Clark, left their home in Ireland and settled in upper Anne Arundel County. It was John R. Clark who gave his family name to Clarksville.[1] The center of Clarksville became established at the corners of Route 108 and Ten Oaks Roads, a few miles north of Highland. Stagecoaches provided transportation to and from Ellicott City. The area was rich in limestone. The following manors and slave quarters provide a glimpse at the way of life for several families during the period of slavery in the county.

FOLLY QUARTER ∾ McTAVISH HOUSE ∾ CARROLLTON MANOR
CLARKSVILLE, MARYLAND

Folly Quarter, also called McTavish House and Carrollton Manor, was built in 1832 by Charles Carroll of Carrollton as a gift to his granddaughter, Emily Caton, who had recently married. The gift was to insure Emily maintained her standard of living. "Folly Quarter contains two basements, one just below ground level, which housed the kitchen and several additional rooms; one still lower, with a wine cellar and servant quarters with several dark rooms intended as dungeons for unruly slaves."[2]

Source: Maryland Historical Trust

54 SEEKING FREEDOM

PERSONAL

RANAWAY from the Subscriber on the 19th instant, a YELLOW MAN, aged 25 years; calls himself JAMES CARR, 6 feet high, slender made, walks lame in the left hip; stoops in the shoulders; occasioned from the lameness of the hip; has small whiskers. Had on when he left home a drab full Linsey frock coat, Osnaburg pants and black fur hat. A REWARD OF FIFTY DOLLARS will be given for the return of said runaway to PHILIP CISSEL, Clarksville, Md., or lodged in jail that I may get him.

HOBBS REGULATION
CLARKSVILLE, MARYLAND

Hobbs Regulation, built in 1832 is significant both architecturally and historically. It was a working farm during the 18th and 19th centuries. This was the home of descendants of John and Dorothy Hobbs of England. "Once known as Rocky Glen, Hobbs Regulation retains a number of the original buildings, including the first residence, a two-room log cabin, a smokehouse, ice house and slave quarters."[3] The U.S. Census of 1790 recorded three slaves living in Hobbs Regulation. In 1797, seven years later, a contract of indenture to Charles Carroll recorded well over 100 slaves. "The War between the States brought unparalleled stress to Hobbs Regulation with regard to the issue of slavery, so the decision was made to grant the slaves their freedom before it became mandatory."

PLANTATION HOUSES IN HOWARD COUNTY 55

COLUMBIA

Columbia, the newest city in Howard County sits side by side with Ellicott City, the oldest city. Columbia was established in 1967. James Rouse and Company built Columbia with the vision of a planned community where descendants of slaves and descendants of Puritans could co-exist as equals. Although Columbia is a little over thirty-three years old, many of the mansions and slave quarters built in the 19th century still remain.

ARLINGTON — COLUMBIA, MARYLAND

Arlington is currently the club house at the Fairway Hills Golf Course (previously Allview Golf Course).
Arlington's early history is obscure, but it has an interesting legend attached to the three-story house:

It is said that for the construction of the main wing
a circular scaffold was erected around the walls as they rose,
with the stones being pushed one by one
up the steep incline and into position.
The work was done single-handedly by an anonymous slave who,
upon its completion was given his freedom.
Time involved for the feat is unknown,
nor is it known how many years of freedom were earned
by the energetic black man.[5]

Source: Maryland Historical Trust

BLANDAIR ROUTE 175
COLUMBIA, MARYLAND

Blandair, located on a tract of land once a part of "Talbott's Resolution Manor," originally comprised 1,987 acres. The estate, now only three hundred acres, is still surrounded by the original simple log house, once used for a smoke house and a stone and frame barn. Northeast of these two buildings lies a gabled roof one-and-a-half story high log house with a central square brick chimney. This building was once used as slave quarters.

THE EYE OF THE CAMEL
COLUMBIA, MARYLAND

The Eye of the Camel was built around 1820. It is cited as a significant building for Howard County and the State of Maryland. Historically it is associated with Oakland Manor, residence of Robert Oliver who built Oliver's Carriage House nearby. It may once have been connected to Oakland Manor by a wide stone passage.

PLANTATION HOUSES IN HOWARD COUNTY 57

LINDEN GROVE
COLUMBIA, MARYLAND

Linden Grove was built by Captain John Worthington Dorsey in 1817. Linden Grove remains a reminder of the original character of old Howard County. It is particularly noteworthy for its association with the Dorsey family of Anne Arundel and Howard Counties. An interesting note about Linden Grove was at one time the attic was completely opened with spinning wheels where slave women spun the thread which made the garments for the slaves. Mary Ann Hammond Dorsey spent much of her time among the whirring wheels overseeing the very productive work in this part of the house.

OAKLAND MANOR
COLUMBIA, MARYLAND

The area surrounding Oakland was originally surveyed by John Dorsey in 1688, before Howard County was formed, and known as Felicity. Two houses stood on the property, one of log and stone and the other only of log. In 1811, Robert Oliver constructed Oakland (known as Oakland Manor) as a country home. Oakland Manor Farm Quarters were built before 1800 (now located on the Ralston House property). "These Quarters may have been the original stone building on this track of land."[7] The quarters were used as a tenant house for Oakland Manor. Later, the Gaither family acquired the property in 1838. One ironic and highly contradictory legend persists: namely, that the manor served as a stop on the Underground Railroad for runaway slaves. This allegation has appeared in a number of accounts of the history of Oakland Manor.

THE RALSTON HOUSE AND SLAVE QUARTERS
ORIGINALLY PART OF THE
OAKLAND MANOR PROPERTY
COLUMBIA, MARYLAND

The old stone house was built before 1820. It faces west on the east side of Hyla Brook Road. A stone slave quarters lies only six inches north of the building's south wall and was connected to the main house by an underground passage. The building remains in a good state of repair. "The blacksmith shop and former slave quarters are now individually owned. The two barns and springhouse are located within the Wilde Lake Park area."

WAVELAND — COLUMBIA, MARYLAND

Waveland is an old Howard County tract located in Sewell's Orchard off Oakland Mills Road in Columbia, Maryland. Waveland was a New Year's Eve gift to Charles Carroll and Edward Dorsey from then Lord Proprietary in 1726. Larkin Dorsey built Waveland, the home, in the early 1800's.

"The Dorsey family had Confederate sympathies; in fact, it is said that this one family furnished more men for the militia than any other in the state. During the war, Northern troops came to the property to appropriate horses; and an old slave on the property had the ability of foretelling such visits and would drive the animals off and hide them until the Yankees had departed."[9] "In 1837, Waveland's twenty-two Negroes were set free."[10]

PLANTATION HOUSES IN HOWARD COUNTY

WOODLAWN FARMS AND SLAVE QUARTERS
COLUMBIA, MARYLAND

Woodlawn Farms Slaves Quarters is believed to have been built by Dr. Allen Thomas. In 1848, Major Henry Howard Owings, one of the first commissioners of Howard County, bought Woodlawn Farms. At one time, the site was part of the Columbia Horse Center. It is now privately owned and its old slave quarters stand unoccupied on the outskirts of three adjacent horse barns which lie south of the main house. Auxiliary buildings and horse barns, including slave quarters and tenant houses, are located east of the property. Woodlawn Farms is described as "one of Howard County's loveliest landmarks, which has remained virtually untouched through the years." [11]

$150 REWARD

RANAWAY from the subscriber, living near Clarksville in Howard District, on Saturday night, the 18th instant, a bright Mulatto MAN named HAZEL SNOWDEN, about 35 years of age, and about 5 feet 10 inches high—has a scar on the right side of the head near the crown. He had on when he left a drab box coat and drab pantaloons, of homespun striped lindsey yeat; pair of new country made boots and a fur hat a little worn. I will give $100 if taken in the State of Maryland and $150 if taken out of the State and secured so that I get him again.

PHILIP SMALLWOOD
CLARKSVILLE, Howard County, Md.

Source: Maryland Historical Trust

Courtesy: Fred Dorsey

60   SEEKING FREEDOM

COOKSVILLE

Cooksville was founded in 1802 by Thomas Cook. As was true of most of Howard County, Cooksville was rural in character and covered with farmlands. A part of the Lisbon Region, it is located in the fourth district near the Carroll County border.

MT. GREGORY METHODIST CHURCH AND COOKSVILLE HIGH
COOKSVILLE, MARYLAND

Mt. Gregory United Methodist Church was organized in 1870, one of the oldest churches in Howard County. Cooksville High, the first Black high school, was also located on this site.

Source: Maryland Historical Trust

DAISY

Daisy was named by Sen. Arthur Pue Gorman after his daughter Grace "Daisy" Gorman. Daisy is southeast of Lisbon, off Frederick Road. The town's main attraction was Oakdale, the mansion of Edwin Warfield, governor of Maryland from 1904 to 1908. Some of the black families who settled in and around Daisy had relatives who had worked as slaves for Governor Warfield.[12]

OAKDALE TENANT HOUSE (LOG HOUSE & WASH HOUSE) AND OAKDALE ~ DAISY, MARYLAND

Oakdale, Daisy's biggest estate, was built before the community received its name. Oakdale was built in 1838 by Albert Gallatin Warfield. When the son, Edwin, inherited Oakdale upon the death of his parents, he enlarged the house, added huge columns on the front and added three side porches around the house. It is said that Albert Warfield was not a man in favor of slavery; in fact, he "established a custom of freeing his slaves on their 40th birthdays, although he needed their labor for the success of his farm."[13]

62 SEEKING FREEDOM

ELKRIDGE

Elkridge, earlier known as both Elk Ridge and Elk Ridge Landing, claims to be the oldest settlement in Howard County. In 1734, the Act of the Assembly established a town at Elk Ridge Landing. "Elk Ridge Landing referred to the shipping docks and concentration of population along the Patapsco River while Elk Ridge referred to a ridge line stretching west to Doughoregan Manor and south to Oakland Mills."[14] In 1835, the Thomas Viaduct was built which provided a railway route to deliver the tobacco, granite, and iron products. The Viaduct also established Elkridge as a focal point of travel to Baltimore and Philadelphia. The culverts or drains in the viaduct served as hiding places for runaway slaves and the railway route provided a means of escape. The following plantation houses in Elkridge still exist.

Source: Maryland Historical Trust

ARMAGH
GEORGE DOBBIN HOUSE
ELKRIDGE, MARYLAND

*The Armagh/Dobbin House is still in existence
It is on the National Register of Historic Places under
the Maryland Historical Trust.
Named for Judge George Washington Dobbin
Armagh was built by Judge Dobbin in the
early 1860's for his son Robert.
The slave quarters were located in the basement.
It is currently occupied by a family whose members
are not descendants of the first owners.*

PLANTATION HOUSES IN HOWARD COUNTY

BELMONT ~ ELKRIDGE, MARYLAND

Belmont was built in 1737 by Caleb Dorsey. The original brick structure, covered with plaster, is an early Elkridge dwelling. What might be of significance is that the stone foundation reveals a tunnel which passed under the east hyphen from the central foyer to the dining room for the use of servants. While the term "servant" was not usually applied to slaves, it is possible that the tunnel may have provided access to the outside as a means of escape. "When Caleb Dorsey died in 1772, he was a wealthy man, owning 3,000 acres and 94 slaves." [15]
"The slaves performed all the agricultural labor." [16]
Belmont is currently owned by the American Chemical Society and serves as a small conference center.

CLOVER HILL ~ ELKRIDGE, MARYLAND

Clover Hill was patented in 1732 by Edward Dorsey and E. Dorsey, Jr. Clover Hill was a 260-acre parcel of land which included portions of "Troy", in addition to "Herbert's Care" and "Dorsey's Inheritance." Clover Hill was built in 1767 by Michael Scott, a tanner, and inherited by his son George Scott in 1770. Thomas and Eleanor Lee, of Virginia, acquired the property in 1788. It is presently owned by Howard County.

HOCKLEY GRIST HOUSE — ELKRIDGE, MARYLAND

This house stands as the remaining building once a part of the Hockley Grist Mill. It is believed to be one of eight of the oldest homes in Howard County. The slave quarters and south wing were the first structures and the two mid-sections later filled in the house. "In the cellar beneath the present kitchen door, which enters into the living room, is a small window through which food was passed. A round well is located north of the west end of the original buildings north wall. A tunnel from the river passed by the well and into the basement kitchen. Water could be drawn from this well at the basement level." The recorded information of the actual location of the enslaved as related to the architecture of the house speaks for itself. It would have been possible for slaves to escape via the trains on the Thomas Viaduct only a few hundred feet from the house.

Source: Maryland Historical Trust

Source: Maryland Historical Trust

TROY HILL — ELKRIDGE, MARYLAND

On November 10, 1695, John Dorsey patented (a term used for land grants by Lord Baltimore before deeds to property was instituted by law) Troy, (the original name of the lands) which consisted of over 1000 acres. It is where he built a house and moved his family. "Most of the interior woodwork remains from the 1830's when it replaced the original after a fire."[30] The house was built of stone. The Dorsey family was one of the largest slave owners in Howard County.

ELLICOTT CITY

Established four years before the United States, Ellicott City is the county seat in Howard County. It sits side by side with the newest city in the county, Columbia, Maryland. "Ellicott City was established in 1772 by three Quaker brothers, Joseph, John and Andrew Ellicott. The three brothers moved from Bucks County, Pennsylvania to Maryland and purchased land on the east of the Patapsco River."[18] The Ellicotts opened a quarry, merchant flour mill, helped build a Quaker meeting house, a school and many houses. Benjamin Banneker, a free black during that time, was befriended by Andrew Ellicott's son, George. Banneker aided George's cousin Andrew in the early surveying of the District of Columbia. Banneker wrote President Thomas Jefferson and questioned his stance on slavery. Many of its 19th century structures remain.

Maryland, Baltimore County, Near Ellicott's Lower Mills
August 19th, 1791

Thomas Jefferson Secretary of State.

Sir, I am fully sensible of the greatness of that freedom which I take with you on the present occasion; a liberty which Seemed to me Scarcely allowable, when I reflected on that distinguished, and dignifyed station in which you Stand; and the almost general prejudice and prepossession which is so previlent in the world against those of my complexion.

I suppose it is a truth too well attested to you, to need a proof here, that we are a race of Beings who have long laboured under the abuse and censure of the world, that we have long been looked upon with an eye of contempt, and that we have long been considered rather as brutish than human, and Scarcely capable of mental endowments.

Sir, I hope I may Safely admit, in consequence of that report which hath reached me, that you are a man far less inflexible in Sentiments of this nature, than many others; that you are measurably friendly and well disposed towards us, and that you are willing and ready to Lend your aid and assistance to our relief from those many distresses and numerous calamities to which we are reduced.

Now, Sir, if this is founded in truth, I apprehend you will readily embrace every opportunity to eradicate that train of absurd and false ideas and oppinions which so generally prevail with respect to us, and that your Sentiments are concurrent with mine, which are that one universal Father hath given being to us all, and that he hath not only made us all of one flesh, but that he hath also without partiality afforded us all the Same Sensations, and endued us all with the same faculties, and that however variable we may be in Society or religion, however diversified in Situation or color, we are all of the Same Family, and Stand in the Same relation to him.

Sir, if these are Sentiments of which you are fully persuaded, I hope you cannot but acknowledge, that it is the indispensible duty of those who maintain for themselves the rights of human nature, and who profess the obligations of Christianity, to extend their power and influence to the relief of every part of the human race, from whatever burthen or oppression they may unjustly labour under; and this I apprehend a full conviction of the truth and obligation of these principles would lead all to…

Benjamin Banneker

First and second pages of Banneker's letter to Thomas Jefferson Dated August 19, 1791, Library of Congress, Manuscripts Division.

66 SEEKING FREEDOM

AVOCA AND AVOCA SLAVE QUARTERS — ELLICOTT CITY, MARYLAND

Avoca stands on part of "Chews Resolution Manor," patented in 1695 by Samuel Chew and comprised of twelve hundred acres. Dr. Arthur Pue of Baltimore City, acquired the property in 1802. Avoca was owned by his son Dr. Michael Pue. Avoca's buildings were constructed in three sections. "The north wall of the house shows a line between the old stone house and a connector is very well marked up to the projecting stone lintel of the second floor window of the early west wing or kitchen wing. Here it stops, leading us to believe that the early structure was a two story high dependency of some sort, probably for slave quarters or food storage, because bars are located in the cellar window."[19] The slave quarters still remain on the premises.

BETHESDA — ELLICOTT CITY, MARYLAND

"Bethesda is situated on land that was part of Chew's Resolution Manor, Long Reach, Search Enlarged and Dorsey's Search. Dr. Michael Pue and Mary Dorsey, Pue built the center portion of this large house in the 1770's after their marriage. A grandson, Henry Hill Pue, built the grand section on the west."[20] The property today consists of three joined wings—the center or oldest fieldstone section (1682), the second section or main wing, and a third wing—a composite of three distinct periods. In addition to the main house are former slave quarters, a stable, and the original smoke house.

PLANTATION HOUSES IN HOWARD COUNTY

DOUGHOREGAN MANOR
ELLICOTT CITY, MARYLAND

"Doughoregan Manor borders a part of Route 144, which was the first section of Frederick Pike, the original roadbed having been laid by slave labor." [21]

"Doughoregan Manor was built about 1730 by Charles Carroll of Annapolis. His son, Charles Carroll of Carrollton, was last of the signers of the Declaration of Independence to survive." [22] Carroll became an anti-slave advocate after signing the Declaration of Independence. The manor has a reputation of being the most famous colonial estate in Maryland.

GRAY ROCK AND GRAY ROCK SLAVE QUARTERS
ELLICOTT CITY, MARYLAND

The history of Gray Rock is tied to the history of the Dorsey family whose members owned numerous tracts of land throughout Howard County. The first documented owner of Gray Rock was Thomas Beale Dorsey, Jr. Gray Rock was located just south of his brother Caleb's estate, "Three Brothers." Slave quarters still remain on the premises.

LINWOOD (LINWOOD CHILDREN'S CENTER)
ELLICOTT CITY, MARYLAND

Linwood, one of the most historic homes still standing in Ellicott City, is located at the terminus of Church Road. It was alleged to have been built in part by slave labor in the mid 1800's. Today the estate serves as the Linwood Children's Center.

MOUNT JOY AND SLAVE QUARTERS
ELLICOTT CITY, MARYLAND

Mount Joy, the main body of the house, was constructed by Dr. Arthur Pue, Jr., about 1813. Samuel Wethered, Jr. lived there and he led pack trains to the southwest where he became a great friend of Kit Carson and acquired his nickname "Sante Fe Sam."[23] Two slave cabins remain at the manor. The one made of stone has a summer kitchen on the ground floor and a separate staircase that slaves would have climbed to the loft upstairs. The wood cabin directly beside it has a log-cabin foundation, and was possibly the original homestead on the farm.[24]

PLANTATION HOUSES ⊣ HOWARD COUNTY

$30 REWARD

RANAWAY from Charlotte A. Tasewell at Ellicott's Mills, a bright MULATTO GIRL, named Sarah Jane. She is about 14 years of age, large black eyes, marked with the small pox, two cuts on her head; she wore away a new blue domestic frock and a white apron. The above reward will be given if taken in the State, or Fifty Dollars if taken out of the State, if returned to Mrs. WATERS, Caroline St. All persons are forewarned against harboring the said girl under the penalty of the law.

Source: Maryland Historical Trust

THE OAKS MANOR HOUSE AND LOG HOUSE
ELLICOTT CITY, MARYLAND

The history of the Oaks is obscured. An article on The Oaks appeared in the Sunday Sun *(circa 1940) which mentioned both Tyson and Ellicott in connection with the early history of the house. A small slave house east of the manor may have been built during the tenure of the Hopkins family.*[25] *The Oaks is at the former site of an Indian Trail.*

In 1852, Robert H. Hare designed and constructed the Oaks while living in Linwood in Ellicott City. The age old Clagget Road was used to haul building materials to the site from the B&Q Railroad Switch. On the Martinet's 1860 map of Howard County, Maryland, Hare is identified as owner of the Oaks. He and his wife Caroline lived there for some six years.

On August 31, 1864, Thomas Donaldson, Trustee, et al granted and conveyed the Oaks, then called 'Mount Misery' and 'Oella Enlarged' to Jehanne Elvira Hopkins. The Hopkins came north with their slaves from the south. Jehanne, wife of Edward Hopkins, had a ninety-nine-year lease on the Oaks which unequivocally stated that it was owned in her own right "regardless of any present or future husband."[26]

Source: Maryland Historical Trust

70   SEEKING FREEDOM

Source: Maryland Historical Trust

Source Maryland Historical Trust

SPRING HILL
ELLICOTT CITY, MARYLAND

"Spring Hill is important, architecturally and historically. Part of a tract known as "Rebecca's Lot," Spring Hill was the gift of Caleb Dorsey, of Belmont, to his daughter Rebecca who married Capt. Charles Ridgely, the builder of Hampton in Baltimore County."[27] Spring Hill is among the county's more prominent haunted houses.

$400 REWARD

RANAWAY from the subscriber, living near Ellicott's Mills, in Howard District, on Saturday night, the 18th inst., the four following NEGROES, viz: Robert, Adam, Sam and Till. ROBERT is a dark mulatto man about 25 years of age, stout made, 5 feet 10 or 11 inches high; has a large mouth, thick lips, and a sluggish walk; a very innocent smile and but little beard; took a variety of clothing, among which was a kind of a blue frock coat and blue pantalets.
ADAM is short and a little darker in color; about 20 or 21 years old, 5 feet 4 or 5 inches high, pleasant look; shows his teeth and the white of his eyes; lisps some when talking; clothing not known.
SAM is darker in color than either of the above; 19 years old; 5 feet 8 inches high. He is slender made, and rather a down look; frowns some when spoken to.
TILL is a large dark mulatto Woman, between 30 and 35 years of age, 5 feet 4 inches high; good looking and very pleasant when spoken to; clothes not known. Robert went in company with 6 or 8 others, among which was a black woman he claimed as his wife.
I will give $50 for each of the above negroes taken within the State or $100 for each if taken out of the State and lodged in any jail within the State, so that I get them again.
REUBEN M. DORSEY,
3 miles above Ellicott's Mills

PERSONAL

— RANAWAY on the 21st March, ed boy, named BENJAMIN COOK, s old, an apprentice to the g business. All persons are inst harboring him, as the enforced against them. The ut no charges, will be paid returning him to me.
James BRICARD,
Ellicott's Mills

SPRING HILL QUARTERS
ELLICOTT CITY, MARYLAND

Spring Hill Quarters, located north of Spring Hill, is a small stone house which served at one time as a slave stockade and later as a tenant cottage. The 30-foot-square stone dwelling is now separated from the Spring Hill Manor and must be approached from New Cut Road. "The earthen floor and wooden slave cells remained untouched until 1914."[28] The Quarters have been converted to a tenant cottage.

Source: Maryland Historical Trust

THE THOMPSON FARM OUTBUILDINGS
ELLICOTT CITY, MARYLAND

"The Thompson Farm Outbuildings are notable, historically and architecturally, to Howard County and the State of Maryland. Historically, they adjoin Doughoregan Manor and are located on the northwest corner of Route 108 and Manor Lane. It leads to the old estate of Charles Carroll of Carrollton. Architecturally, the dairy is representative of the fine stone buildings which are found throughout Howard County and which feature field stone quoining, projecting stone sills and flat stone lintels as well as fine scale and proportions. An interesting water trough is featured here. The nineteenth century two story high, frame building, is believed to have been used as slave quarters." [29]

PERSONAL

$50 REWARD—Absconded from the farm of the subscriber, on Elkridge, Howard District, Anne Arundel county, on the night of the 16th inst., a Negro Man, named **JACOB CASSEL** or **CASTLE**. He is black, supposed to be about 21 years of age, 5 feet, 9 or 10 inches high, strong, hearty, and indeed a powerful negro. He has no particular marks and his appearance proves the fact of the kind treatment he has always received. His ears have been bared and he wears strings in them. His working clothes consisted of Russia sheeting jacket and trowsers, and his shirts of twilled cotton of the best quality. He took with him all his clothing, a description of which cannot be given, as he has several suits. He was charged on yesterday by Beale Whalen, who resides at Marriottsville, with having aided and assisted his woman named Fanny Smith, in making her escape on Sunday night last; no other cause can be assigned for his running away, and as no threats of punishment were made, it is presumed a consciousness of guilt or discovery must have prompted him.

Jacob has a mother named Suck, whose husband is named Kit or Christopher Cassel or Castle, both of whom reside at or near Ellicott's Mills. He has many acquaintances in Baltimore, a brother named William or Bill, who, it is said, is or was in the employment of Messrs. Hopkins & Brothers.

The above reward will be paid on his delivery to me, or my manager, Mr. Nicholas Lusby. It is believed that Jacob will endeavor to make his way to Pennsylvania, or that he will be found in the city of Baltimore.

WM H. MARRIOTT,
Woodford Farm, July 17th 1840.

GLENELG

Glenelg is one of the early rural communities settled in Howard County and acquired its name from nearby historic Glenelg Manor. In the nineteenth century, Gen. Joseph Tyson acquired the property and built a large stone dwelling modeled after a castle of the Tudor Period, to which he gave the name Glenelg. According to the 1878 Maryland Directory, Glenelg had a healthy population of 75 persons.

Source: Maryland Historical Trust

THE HERBIARY
GLENELG, MARYLAND

The original eighteenth century, one-story high, gabled roof, fieldstone building faces south with a wide brick chimney inset into its west wall. The chimney holds a large cooking fireplace. The original kitchen may be dated as early as 1760. Pottery, old glass and remnants of old hurricane lamps have been found on the site.[32] The foundation for the old slave quarters lies south of the main house and presently is the site of a vegetable garden. The Hall House, located on the opposite side of the Herbiary, has an identical plan to the slave house once located there.

PLANTATION HOUSES IN HOWARD COUNTY 73

GLENWOOD

Historically, in 1822, Glenwood was known as Matthews Post Office of Anne Arundel County, and more simply "Matthews". "James B. Matthews and his wife, Kitty Griffith Matthews, were the founders of the community known today as Glenwood. They operated a store and post office."[33] James became the postmaster. Lycurgus Matthews, son of James and Kitty, operated a private school, the Glenwood Institute. Thus the name was applied to the community.

CATTAIL FARM — GLENWOOD, MARYLAND

"Historically, this property is one of the most interesting in Howard County because it is connected with the prominent Banks family, who settled "New Year's Gift" in the first half of the nineteenth century."[34] It has been noted that by 1856, the year of Samuel Banks' will, he had accumulated some 900 acres of land and owned some 34 slaves.

Source: Maryland Historical Trust

74 SEEKING FREEDOM

ELLERSLIE
GLENWOOD, MARYLAND

Ellerslie is located on the east side of Route 97 opposite Union Chapel. The original or eastern portion of the house was erected about 1792 by Captain Henry Ridgely. Ellerslie had its beginning as a two-room hunting lodge. Standing on a tract of over 100 acres, it is surrounded by a spring house, an old log house, barns and out buildings, some of which may well antedate the building. The western, or new portion, of the house, almost a duplicate of the original half, was added by Basil Crapster about the middle of the nineteenth century. Ellerslie is located on lands which are a portion of a large tract called Ridgely's Great Range.[36] In addition, there is a passageway that is said to have been used by slaves in their escape.

Source: Maryland Historical Trust

Source: Maryland Historical Trust

OLD WILSON PLACE AT ROXBURY MILL
GLENWOOD, MARYLAND

The old Wilson Place was built in 1847. It is associated with Allen Bowie Davis who owned this property in 1859. "Wilson Place is located in the thriving nineteenth century community of Roxbury Mill on the banks of the Cattail River. Architecturally, the frame section of the building is noteworthy and is believed to have been standing in 1859 when Allen Davis conveyed the property to a Mr. Kinsey."[37] The log section is believed to have once been used as slave quarters and was later dismantled and reassembled.

PLANTATION HOUSE IN HOWARD COUNTY 75

HIGHLAND

Highland is four miles west of Fulton and was known originally as Walls' Cross Roads. The name Highland was chosen because of the lay of the land. The plantation house on the right still stands in Highland.

HICKORY RIDGE — HIGHLAND, MARYLAND

Hickory Ridge is one of the original homes in Highland. Built by Greenberry Ridgely, it stands on the northwestern fringe of Highland. "A sizeable stone slave cabin, believed to date from the mid-18th century, has been converted into a handsome cottage." [38]

Source: Maryland Historical Trust

LAUREL

The history of Laurel has its beginnings in 1686 when land was granted to Richard Snowden "By the early 19th century, around 1812, Laurel served as a major stage coach stop between the cities of Baltimore and Washington."[39] There were no plantations. Its earliest history includes the establishment of mills to produce cotton fabrics. During the height of its activity five hundred people were employed–African Americans were excluded from employment.

A WORTHINGTON RESIDENCE ~ LAUREL, MARYLAND

Dr. Thomas Chew Worthington, a physician in Baltimore who resided in Howard County, purchased this residence in 1845. The original house, it has been noted by historians, in an examination of the basement, reveals what once might have been a root cellar. Below the kitchen is a place for storage, or prison for slaves.

Source: Maryland Historical Trust

A WORTHINGTON LOG HOUSE ~ LAUREL, MARYLAND

It is believed that the original section of this log house was an early settlers' home (ante bellum). The residence's original and present kitchen section stems from circa 1709 when John Warfield and his wife Rachel acquired the property. The log house, along with the residence, stood on the most northern survey of Warfield's Range. In 1845, when Dr. Thomas Worthington acquired the property, the northern addition to the cabin was added. It has hand-hewn supporting beams for the upstairs loft rather than logs, and the planks of the loft were random width, almost half the width of the extremely wide planks used for the loft flooring of the south side of the cabin. Originally in North Laurel, the building was moved in 1996 to Rockburn Branch Park in Elkridge. Known as the Warfield, Phelps and Gorman cabin for its owners, the settlers' home was also a possible slave cabin.

PLANTATION HOUSES ~ HOWARD COUNTY 77

LISBON

Lisbon was founded in the early 1800's as a farming village and supply depot. It served as a way station for stagecoach and wagon travelers who journeyed on the old Frederick Turnpike. Caleb Pancoast is credited with founding the town. He built the first house in Lisbon around 1810. "History records that General Lafayette visited Lisbon in 1824 on his way to Frederick, Maryland. He was cheered on by both children and adults as a revolutionary war hero."[40] Although the area did not have plantations for an enslaved population, they were, for the most part sympathetic to the Confederate cause. Many 19th century structures remain including three houses only 13 feet wide built 133 years ago.

Source: Maryland Historical Trust

THE FLOHR-BARNES HOUSE
LISBON, MARYLAND

The Flohr-Barnes House is situated north on the south side of Route 144, some 70 feet east of the intersection of Route 94 and Route 144.[41] *The Flohr-Barnes house was built in the early 19th century, with construction completed around 1812. The house is so named after two of its owners, The Flohr and the Barnes families. "It has a very interesting southern wing of brick which is presently used for storage, but may at one time have been a detached kitchen and/or slave quarters for the main residence."*[42]

MARRIOTTSVILLE

Before the late 17th century, the valley of Marriottsville belonged to the Indians. "Historians place the valley within the territorial hunting grounds of the Susquehannocks; to the south, were the villages of the Piscataways."[13] "This town derived its name from the Marriott family, founded by John Marriott who settled into Anne Arundel in circa 1664. A son, Richard Marriott, gave the family name to this small town."[4] "The exact date of settlement is unknown, but postal records indicate it did exist in the 1850s."[5] During the Civil War the area was known to Confederate soldiers who destroyed railroad tracks and bridges.

IVY HILL — MARRIOTTSVILLE, MARYLAND

Originally, Ivy Hill was part of the Marriott plantation which became known as Marriottsville. The Howard line of Marriotts stemmed from John Marriott II, who married Elizabeth Davis, daughter of Richard Davis of Ranter's Ridge. Their son, Richard Davis Marriott married Sarah Hammond and they were the parents of the celebrated General William Hammond Marriott, commanding officer of the Anne Arundel County militia in the War of 1812. He had a large home where the Sisters of Bon Secours have their retreat house south of Ivy Hill, which was at one time either a tenant house or dower house for General Marriott. The date, 1811, has been placed on the stone base below the eaves of the roof. It may well be that he built and lived in this field stone house and later moved to his grander home, which has since been leveled.

Source: Maryland Historical Trust

PLANTATION HOUSES IN HOWARD COUNTY 79

THE ROLAND MAXWELL FARMHOUSE
MARRIOTTSVILLE, MARYLAND

Historically, the Roland Maxwell Farmhouse is associated with Robert Stuart Maxwell and his wife, Mary Jane Devries. Robert and Mary moved into the original section of the house and later enlarged it. Their son, Roland Maxwell, was born in the house and later made it home. "Architecturally, the building is noteworthy. An early section is reputed to have been used as slave quarters for Waverly."[46]

WAVERLY
MARRIOTTSVILLE, MARYLAND

Waverly, home of Governor George Howard, is located on the east side of Marriottsville Road. "Approached by a quarter mile long private drive, the mansion commands a magnificent vista of the immediate countryside."[47] *Other sites on the property include what once was one of several log slave quarters. Of this particular structure only the foundations and chimney base remain. About one hundred yards southwest of the house is the shattered tombstone of John Eager Howard, a son of George Howard, former governor, who died in 1838. Although the stone is still on the property, the body was moved to Frederick, Maryland many years ago.*

SYKESVILLE

"James Sykes from England gave his name to Sykesville after settling in the Howard area. He purchased a mill on the upper Patapsco River." [48] The mill was converted from grain to cotton but was not a success. "On January 2, 1851 Judge Thomas Beale Dorsey, a delegate, presented the petition of James Sykes and others asking that the Howard District of Anne Arundel County be established as a new county, to be known as Howard County." [49] The petition was approved and Howard County was established in 1851.

SALOPHA ~ SYKESVILLE, MARYLAND

The original "Salopha" was granted to John Johnson from the King of England on September 18, 1742. Joshua Dorsey Warfield later inherited the property that consisted of a 340-acre plantation. His property included "Belts Hills" an eight hundred acre tract, patented by Benjamin Belts on July 10, 1723. A myth persists that an early owner negotiated with the Indians to buy the farm. "The question, 'Did Benjamin Belts brother, John ever buy the land from the Indians?' remains a mystery." [50]

Several wills found on the property by the current owner note the following: The will of John Dorsey, December 27, 1750 bequeaths Belt Hills to John's son Vachel, along with the slaves Sam, Robin, James, Rose, Abigail, Sam the son of Rose and Fanney. The will of Vachel Dorsey, probated on March 9, 1798 bequests the following slaves to Vachel's daughter Ruth Owings, or if she had predeceased him to his granddaughter Ruth and Mariah Rachel and her increase; Jacob (a lad) and Saul (a boy), Nels (a girl) and her increase. (Ruth Owings did not predecease her father.)

PLANTATION HOUSES IN HOWARD COUNTY

WOODBINE

Woodbine was developed because of its close proximity to the Patapsco River and the Mainline of the B&O Railroad. Canneries were a business venture offered to immigrant workers and others in the community. Woodbine is associated with the Warfield family who established Cherry Grove and Sunny-Side plantations. In 1855, it is reported that William Henry Smith, a free black man, bought one and a half acres of land in this area. He paid $15 for the property and sold it eight years later for $100. This caused some turbulence in the county.

ALBERT WARFIELD TENANT HOUSE
WOODBINE, MARYLAND

The Albert Warfield Tenant House was built in 1750. This black tenant house offers an example of a comfortable, well heated, frame house with central staircase and upstairs bedrooms which provided housing to those black families associated with Oakdale.[51] Architecturally, it demonstrates the extension of existing building as a common practice to accommodate growing families.

Source: Maryland Historical Trust

CHERRY GROVE
WOODBINE, MARYLAND

Cherry Grove was considered the seat of the Warfield families. After acquiring the land in 1755, a central section was built in 1768. Ten years before the advent of the Revolutionary War, Benjamin Warfield bought an area known as Fredericksburg, then 520 acres, on which Cherry Grove was built. Enslaved persons operated the farm of the Warfields. Albert G. Warfield, born February 1817 at Cherry Grove, inherited enslaved persons and a portion of his father's plantation on which he built Oakdale.[52]

J. P. TARENZ LOG HOUSE
(CHERRY GROVE SLAVE QUARTERS)
WOODBINE, MARYLAND

The J. P. Tarenz Log House faces north on the west side of Duval Road, three-tenths of a mile north of its intersection with Edward Warfield Road. It was originally part of the Cherry Grove Slave Quarters. One of several log cabins constructed in 1768 by Benjamin Warfield, it was moved from its original site after the Civil War. It has been incorporated into the present residence of Mr. and Mrs. Timourian, who painted the log house white. Architecturally, it is a fine example of an eighteenth or early nineteenth century log slave cabin. The J. P. Tarenz Log House is one the cabins which after the Civil War were given to the freed slaves and moved from its original site.

PLANTATION HOUSES IN HOWARD COUNTY   83

Source: Maryland Historical Trust

THE RUTH DAGGETT HOUSE
WOODBINE, MARYLAND

The Ruth Daggett House is associated with Shipley's Discovery Plantation and with a free black man, William Henry Smith. In 1855, Thomas Barnes conveyed one and one-half acres of Shipley's Discovery for $15.00 to William Henry Smith, "together with all singular the tenements, hereditaments and appurtenances thereupon belonging."[53] The simple four-room house is believed to have existed at that time and was renovated, with the central intersecting gable added to its east facade as well as the west wing, which created the "L" plan. William Henry Smith owned the property for eight years and in 1863 sold the property for $100.00.

SUNNYSIDE — WOODBINE, MARYLAND

The Sunnyside Plantation was built in 1800. It is historically significant because it is associated with the Warfield Family of Cherry Grove. Albert Gallatin Warfield, an owner, inherited a large number of slaves and was considered one of the largest slave owners in his section of the state. "Albert was noted as an 'indulgent master' who freed his slaves when they reached the age of forty, believing slavery to be inconsistent with republican institutions. Albert and his brother, Gassaway Watkings Warfield are commemorated on the Confederate Monument in front of the Howard County Court House."[54]

Source: Maryland Historical Trust

References

1. Stein, Charles Francis, Jr., *Origin and History of Howard County, Maryland*, Baltimore: Howard County Historical Society, 1972, Pg. 135-186
2. Holland, Celia, M. *Old Homes and Families of Howard County*, Maryland: Privately Printed, 1987, Pg. 374
3. Ibid, Pg. 275
4. Ibid, Pg. 276
5. Ibid, Pg. 430
6. Ibid, Pg. 363
7. Maryland Historic Trust Sites Inventory Survey, HC-331, Maryland Historic Trust, Peoples Resource Center, Crownsville, Maryland
8. Ibid., HO 184
9. Holland, Pg. 424-425
10. Maryland Historic Trust Sites Inventory Survey, HC-34
11. Ibid., HO-411
12. Thornton, Susan, "Daisy, Daisy," *The Columbia Flyer*, March 14, 1991, p. 31
13. Holland, Celia M. *Old Homes and Families of Howard County, Maryland*: Privately Printed, 1987, pg. 374.
14. "Howard County Area History: Elkridge," www.howardcounty.com/history/html, Pg. 2
15. Holland, Pg. 22
16. Maryland Historical Trust Sites Inventory, HO-43
17. Ibid., HO-152
18. "Ellicott City History," www.visitellicottcity.com/history/default.asp?category=history
19. Maryland Historic Trust Sites Inventory Survey, HO-422
20. Holland, p. 108
21. Maryland Historic Trust Sites Inventory Survey, HO-22
22. Ibid., HO-22
23. Maryland Historic Trust Sites Inventory Survey, HO-145
24. MacGillis, Alec, "Cabin might have housed slaves", *The Howard County Sun*, April 8, 2000, p. 17B.
25. Maryland Historic Trust Sites Inventory, HO-243
26. Ibid., HO-243
27. Ibid., HO-31
28. Holland, Pg. 103
29. Maryland Historic Trust Sites Inventory, HO-477
30. Ibid., HO-44
31. Ibid., Pg. 251
32. Maryland Historic Trust Sites Inventory, Op. Cit, HO-239
33. Cramm, Joetta M., *Howard County, A Pictorial History, Maryland*, p 113
34. Maryland Historic Trust Sites Inventory, Op. Cit, HO-287
35. Ibid., HO-6
36. Stein, Charles Francis, Jr., *Origin and History of Howard County, Maryland*: Howard County Historical Society, 1972, p. 271.
37. Holland, Op. Cit., p. 296
38. Ibid., Pg. 341-342
39. Community Information Guide, City of Laurel, Maryland, 1997
40. Holland, p. 190
41. Maryland Historic Trust Sites Inventory, Op. Cit, HO-196
42. Ibid., Op. Cit, HO-199
43. Holland, p. 440-41, appendix
44. Stein, p. 281-282
45. Holland, p. 158
46. Maryland Historic Trust Sites Inventory, Op. Cit, HO-191
47. National Register of Historic Places, United States Department of the Interior, National Park Service, Howard County, Maryland
48. Stein, Pg. 115
49. Ibid., Pg. 116
50. Maryland Historic Trust Sites Inventory Survey, HO-533
51. Ibid., HO-257
52. Ibid., HO-255
53. Ibid, HO-288
54. Ibid., HO-115

BIBLIOGRAPICAL HIGHLIGHTS

LISTEN CHILDREN

*Listen children
keep this in the place
You have for keeping
always keep it all ways*

We have never hated black

*Listen
We have been ashamed
Hopeless, tired, mad
But always
All ways
We loved us*

*We have always loved each other
Children
All ways
Pass it on*

– Lucille Clifton

JAMES DORSEY ~ 1908

Straight as an arrow, with the voice of an orator, James Dorsey began the story of his life from his birth, in 1908, in the Jonestown area of Howard County. He grew up with his parents, John and Louise Dorsey, and his two brothers and four sisters, in a home in close proximity to the site on which Howard High School now stands. Mr. Dorsey's father was a chauffeur and overseer on the farm of General Charles D. Gaither, the actual site of Howard High School today. His family offered much affection and guidance to offset the difficult times in which he grew up. Though his elementary school was a one-room classroom for all grades, he realized he had been taught well when he later attended Phyllis Wheatley, School #110 in Baltimore, and was well prepared to the extent that, he was advanced half a grade. Mr. Dorsey graduated from Frederick Douglass High School in Baltimore. He entered the Baltimore City Teachers School, now Coppin State College, and pursued a career as a businessman. Before Mr. Dorsey began his business career, he was drafted into the U.S. Army. Upon his return, and with his business training, Mr. Dorsey opened a CITGO service station.

As a widower for the second time, he has devoted his life to activities with the Prince Hall Masons. At 94 years of age, Mr. Dorsey not only looks decades younger, but has the glow of good health. He remembers his maternal grandmother Watkins talking about how, when she was a child, she watched her mother and father, the Webbs, being placed on a wagon to be sold into bondage. She lived to the age of 101 and this event was still vivid in her mind. Grandmother Watkins was a mid-wife and Mr. Dorsey says she delivered all the babies in Howard County. He deplored the overall conditions in existence at the time; and they have never been erased from his memory. "It was a simply dreadful time, what decent people had to undergo." One senses the strong character extending through the pain, the caring of humanity, and his outstanding self-esteem.

BIOGRAPHICAL HIGHLIGHTS

BEULAH MARIE JOHNSON-COOK   1908 – 1999

Beulah Marie Johnson-Cook, born: May 22, 1908, lived at 4987 Green Bridge Road, Dayton, Maryland, since mid-adolescence. When Mrs. Cook was in her mid-twenties, she purchased ten and one-half acres of land on which her home presently rests. Her house is over one-hundred years old, and was initially built for her maternal grandparents, Steven and Eliza Jane Clark, by their employers, the Talbots. Beulah M. Johnson-Cook married Carter Cook in 1926 and had one daughter, Pauline Cook Berry Jones, a former Howard County Colored School valedictorian and retired U.S. government civil servant. Mrs. Cook had six grandchildren and seven great grandchildren.

Mrs. Cook was one of seven children born to Andrew Augustus and Alvina Charlotte Johnson. The significant male family figures in Mrs. Cook's family were fine farmers and blacksmiths. Her mother, Alvina Johnson, was a widely known mid-wife, herbalist, accordion/harmonica player, and member of Brown's Chapel Senior Choir. Mrs. Cook was the eldest member and mother of Brown's Chapel United Methodist Church. She was also a former trustee and Sunday School teacher/treasurer of Brown's Chapel. She retired a domestic worker and former foster home parent. She and her late husband, Carter Cook, were former proprietors of Cook's Baseball Diamond which many people (African American and white) came to from miles around to enjoy baseball games, parades, drive-in movies, cookouts and concerts.

COSETTE HARDING ✻ 1911

YESTERYEAR
By Cosette Harding

How well do I remember
Those days of yesteryear
When Mom and Pop were with us
And we could hear their voices near.

I remember the cow, the horses
chickens, ducks and geese
How we drew the water from the well
And the had time to tease

When at last evening came
And we had time for fun
We would gather around and play some games
For that day's work was done

We would go to bed with the chickens
And get up with the sun
Those old people meant business
I knew them every one

You obeyed your parents and did your chores
Until you became of age
Then it was time to get a job
Because you've turned another page

Born August 14, 1911, Mrs. Cosette Harding talks about her life in Howard County. As a child she remembers bringing water from the spring, and her father bringing the groceries home. Her fondest memories as a child are of the 4th of July, where there was lots of homemade ice cream and cakes, and going to Asbury Methodist Church and Sunday School. Mrs. Harding's mother and sister played the organ and she sang. Her mother, Ida Carroll, had her own cow and made her own butter. Her father, John Carroll, was a B & O Railroad worker. She had five brothers and four sisters, and she was next to the youngest. As they all grew up, her brothers worked for the railroad with their dad, and her sisters did laundry. Mrs. Harding didn't start school until she was eight years old, attending the colored elementary school at Mission Road and Route 32. Once started, she continued school until she graduated from the African American High School, Lakeland, in College Park, Maryland.

She met Charles, her husband in grade school, and married him right after graduating from Lakeland High School on May 15, 1929. In May of 1990 they renewed their vows after celebrating 61 years together. Mr. Harding was a farmer and then a construction worker. Mrs. Harding picked vegetables until she became the first African American cashier at the then segregated Howard High School in Howard County. Mrs. Harding has three children, 18 grandchildren, 19 great-grandchildren, and even one great-great granddaughter. Cosette and Charles Harding joined First Baptist Church of Guilford shortly after their marriage in 1929. "Without the church in my life, I'd feel empty". These days, she is one of the oldest members. For 27 years she served as president of the Missionary Society, and was the first woman on the board of trustees. Mrs. Cosette Harding's life centers around her church and her great admiration of her family.

LEOLA MAY MOORE DORSEY ❧ 1917

Leola May Moore Dorsey was born at home in the small, rural community of Guilford, in Howard County, on August 3, 1917, to Aileen and Henry Moore. Leola was the fourth of ten children. Times were difficult for the African American community and her mother did laundry for people in Savage, grew vegetables, raised chickens for eggs and owned and operated a store on Guilford Road. Leola grew up in segregated Howard County, and attended Robert Guilford Elementary School at Guilford and Missions Roads. Mrs. Dorsey graduated from Booker T. Washington Junior High School, in Baltimore and Lakeland Senior High School in College Park, Maryland. Mrs. Dorsey was able to secure a better paying job than most young African American women in her community. She received $15 a week managing a home for a widowed school teacher and her two daughters. Five dollars was sent home to her mother; another five dollars was saved; and the remaining five dollars covered expenses.

In 1937 Mrs. Dorsey married Remus Dorsey who she describes as "one of the best husbands in the world". She was the assistant manager of Remus' window-washing business and managed the firm after her husband's death in 1974. Their son Charles, now an educator in Calvert County Public Schools, lives in Landover, Maryland, and is the father of five and grandfather of two. He also attended Guilford Elementary. Mrs. Dorsey was active in the county and national PTA's and the first woman elected President of the Howard County Chapter of the National Association for the Advancement of Colored People (NAACP) in May, 1947. She was very involved in the civil rights movement in the late 1950's, campaigning for desegregation in Howard County, especially in schools and restaurants. Mrs. Dorsey joined the First Baptist Church of Guilford, in 1938, and remains a member of the congregation to this day. She was appointed to the board of trustees of Howard Community College in January, 1973 by Governor Harry Hughes and served in that position for nearly 15 years. A beautiful lady, she still lives in the house she and Remus built 52 years ago, on Guilford Road, and continued to work until the age of 83, as site manager for the Guilford senior citizens for the Howard County Office of Aging.

JEANNETTE WILLIAMS RANDALL   1904 – 2001

Jeannette Williams Randall was born on June 1, 1904, the year a fire destroyed much of Baltimore City and the banks where her parents kept their savings. She was born within shouting distance of Locust Chapel in Simpsonville, Maryland, located at Route 29 and Old Route 32 in a log cabin. Mrs. Randall was one of thirteen children, and her loving parents were Ellen Bell and Robert Lee Williams. Ellen Bell worked as a housekeeper for the MacGill family who owned the doughnut factory in Ellicott City and whose property is now King's Contrivance, and she also worked for Senator Arthur Pue Gorman, Jr. Her father, Robert Lee Williams, opened a blacksmith ship in 1885, which operated for 50 years. Mrs. Randall attended Atholton Elementary School from 1909 to 1916. She then went to live with her sister, Mae Emma Campbell (wife of the Mayor of Fairmount Heights), to attend Dunbar High School, from which she graduated in 1925. Jeannette attended the School of Nursing at Howard University. After leaving Howard, Mrs. Randall found work, during the depression, as a child's nurse. She sent money home to help her parents, because no jobs and very little food were available. Everyone used the barter system as much as possible. She also worked in a sewing factory during World War II. In 1930, she married William Henry Randall of Cooksville, Maryland. Mr. Randall was an engineer. They had two children; William Henry, Jr., and Jeanne Ellen.

Mrs. Jeannette Randall was widely known for her beautiful gardens. She first displayed her green thumb talent with the most beautiful "victory garden" in her neighborhood in East Baltimore. In 1946, the family moved to a ninety-three acre farm in Lisbon, Maryland. It was very productive. They also raised chickens. Mrs. Randall distinguished herself as one of the great cooks of the area by winning three Blue Ribbons at the Howard County Fair in 1951. The farm was sold in 1957 and the Randalls became owners of a package goods store. After Mr. Randall's death, Mrs. Randall concentrated on her flowers and culinary delights. She was an active member of the Locust United Methodist Church's Women's Society and was the mother of the Church.

MARY ALMA LOMAX ❧ 1916

Mary Alma Lomax was two years old when World War I started. She and her twin sister lived with their grandmother in Virginia until they were six years old. Mrs. Lomax and her sister moved to Laurel, Maryland to stay with their aunt, uncle and cousin. They lived in a four-room house with a large kitchen. During the day, her uncle used the front room for a barbershop, which both African Americans and white people patronized. He taught her how to cut his hair. The house had a coal/wood burning stove and a water pump outside in the yard. Clothes were washed by hand on a washboard. Her aunt ran their home with strict discipline. They grew their own food, raised and cured hogs, canned foods, and raised chickens. Mrs. Lomax fondly remembers the fried chicken, biscuits, and fruitcake. She was the cook in the house and her sister cleaned.

Mrs. Lomax walked about two miles to a one-room schoolhouse with a big stove in the middle of the room. She graduated after the seventh grade and went to Lakeland High School in Prince George's County, Maryland for African American children. After graduation she married Mr. Lomax from Murkirk, Maryland. She says, "He was my only serious boyfriend". They had two children. Mrs. Lomax entered Federal Government employment in Washington, D.C. as a clerk, went to the Cortez Peters Business School for typing, and was promoted from there on until she retired from government service. During World War II, she worked across the street from the White House. Her sister also worked for the Federal Government in the Internal Revenue Service.

For recreation, there were only church and house parties available in Laurel, Maryland for African Americans unless they went to Washington, D.C. or Baltimore. The city of Laurel did have an Emancipation Celebration Day in September, with rides, games, and food that they all attended. The church provided most of the picnics, ball games, programs, and etc. for recreation. She is a faithful worker in the church, and a life long exemplary member of the Women's Society. Mary Alma Lomax, with strong mind and spirit, continues to enjoy retirement at the age of 85.

MARY JANE SCOTT HOUSTON & 1911

Mary Jane Scott Houston was born January 21, 1911 to Oliver and Carrie Scott. She had sixteen brothers and sisters. She attended the Ellicott City Colored School up to seventh grade. Mrs. Houston loves to cook, and bake cakes. She also worked as a cook for a family in Ellicott City, Maryland. In 1925 she was married to James Edward Henry Houston, from Sykesville, Maryland, whom she says was a very good and loving husband. Mr. Houston worked at the Maryland Mill Supply in Sykesville, Maryland. They had twelve children of which there were two sets of twins. Ten children lived, and they are all living today. While Mrs. Houston was raising her family, her sister died and left five children. Mrs. Houston raised these five children with her own ten. The family lived on Fells Lane until a fire destroyed that house. They then moved to an eleven-room house in Ellicott City, Maryland. This house stands within the boundaries of the Ellicott City Historic District. It has been an integrated neighborhood since the early 1900's. Mrs. Houston continues to live in the house on Frederick Road, with her son William Houston.

Mary Jane Scott Houston was a tireless worker in the St. Luke African Methodist Episcopal Church, Ellicott City, founded in 1877. She sang in the choir, memorized all the hymns, and sang solos. She also remembers fondly how every Sunday after church the family house was the gathering place for family and friends. Everyone brought a dish and the family enjoyed dinner together.

ALBERT E. FRANCE ❧ 1917 – 2001

Albert E. France, born January 5, 1917, was the fourth child of Sara Jane and Louis France. Mr. France lived in the family home on Route 97, Cooksville, Maryland. The log cabin home was built for his great-great grandmother, Sarah Jane Dorsey, after she was freed from slavery in 1860. It has been placed on the National Register of Historic Places in Howard County.

Mr. France left Cooksville in 1942 as an American soldier. He was sent to Alaska as a 25-year old sergeant in the 93rd Engineers Company. Along with 10,000 other American soldiers and civilians he braved temperatures as low as 70 degrees below zero to build a 1,442 mile stretch of roadway to secure a direct road to the United States in case of a Japanese invasion. Known as the Alcan Highway, it took eight months to complete through five mountain ranges and across 100 rivers. Working against time, they carved a highway through the frozen wilderness. Of the 10,000 who worked on the highway, 3,695 African Americans labored with little mention of their participation. Mr. France said, "In those days, they didn't think we were smart enough to do this kind of thing." He spent another two years building runways and roads on the Aleutian Islands. He was later shipped out to the Burma Road in Southeast Asia. On the Alaska Highway's 50th birthday celebration, the African American Soldiers were honored for their participation for the first time.

Mt. Gregory United Methodist Church—built in 1870, also listed on the National Register of Historic Places in Howard County, and seated across the road from Mr. France's log cabin home—honored him in 1993 with an Albert E. France Day. This tribute was for his long and wonderful service in the church. Albert E. France, truly someone to be honored.

ALICE REBECCA DORSEY THOMAS
1908 – 2000

Alice Rebecca Dorsey Thomas was born on September 24, 1908, the sixth child and second daughter born to Mary Stinson and Channing William Dorsey. Becky was born in the house in which she resided until suffering a stroke in May 2000—the house her grandfather and father built in Daisy, Maryland. Becky attended elementary and "middle" school and worshipped at Daisy Church—the church founded by her grandfather. Becky married Even Stanton and moved to Baltimore, Maryland. In 1956, she moved back to her homestead in Howard County and renewed her membership at Daisy Church. She participated in church activities, serving several terms as President of the Women's Society for Christian Service (Methodist Women) and Communion Steward, and served on the church board.

All of her employment was as "downstairs maid" and/or cook for many of Baltimore's wealthiest and influential people. Even though the wages were low, the hours long and work back-breaking, Becky gave 100% plus to each and every job she had.

Becky married twice. Her first marriage was to Even Stanton circa 1924/25 and her second was to Robert Thomas circa 1944/45. Although she was not blessed to have had children of her own, Becky was "second" mother to many and wise counselor to many more.

Cooking and crocheting were the things Becky loved doing and she was excellent at both and had the patience to teach anyone who wanted to learn.

BIOGRAPHICAL HIGHLIGHTS 95

ELIZABETH GARRETT 1914

With a strong clear voice, alive with vitality, Elizabeth Garrett told the story of her life. She was born December 29, 1914 in Birmingham, Alabama to John and Carrie Rummage. Mrs. Garrett's mother taught school and her father was a bricklayer. She had one brother and one sister.

While finishing high school in Birmingham, she transferred to cosmetology in her senior year. She graduated and pursued a career in cosmetology, becoming so skilled in "Marcel Waves" that a lady visiting from Washington, DC offered her a position in Washington. She moved there in 1945. While still in Birmingham, she met and married Melvin Garrett in 1944. They had one son, Samuel. Elizabeth and Melvin came to Washington where they lived for ten years. There Mr. Garrett learned the cooking trade, starting as a dishwasher, he worked his way up to chef. In 1955, Mr. Garrett rented the "Log Cabin" restaurant in Jessup, Maryland. Elizabeth eventually joined him in the restaurant business. In 1962, they were able to purchase the restaurant, and the house next door. They have operated the Log Cabin Restaurant and lived in the house on Washington Boulevard in Jessup, Maryland, for over forty years. Mr. Melvin Garrett died in 1983. Mrs. Garrett continues to operate the restaurant, with the help of her son and Miss Connie Jones who has been a very vital part of the business.

Mrs. Garrett's restaurant has survived in spite of other restaurants moving into the area and has continued with a good popular service. Their specialty is seafood and good home cooked meals of ribs, chitterlings, pork chops, and steaks. At eighty-six years of age, Mrs. Garrett is still working part time in the business. She says, "My husband and I had always planned to sell the business and have some time to enjoy life, which we never did. I have no regrets. It's been a good life."

96 SEEKING FREEDOM

AGNES ODELLA SMITH HOLLAND ❧ 1911

Agnes Odella Smith Holland was born and raised in Cooksville, Howard County, Maryland, on June 4, 1911. She is one of the eleven children of late Josephine Prettyman Smith (direct descendant of a Cherokee Indian tribe) and Caleb Smith. Her surviving siblings include two sisters, Sadie Fisher of Brooklyn, New York and Harriett Jackson of Baltimore, Maryland and two brothers: Nathan Smith of Cooksville, Maryland, and Paul Smith of Highland, Maryland. As a child, she attended Cooksville Elementary School in the small rural town of Cooksville, in Howard County, Maryland. Her favorite teacher was Ms. Nina Meadows, and she loved to recount stories about her, especially of that teacher's strict discipline to her children. Agnes soon learned domestic chores and grew to love cleaning and caring for children, which she did later in life for other people. She has always been known for her neat, clean home.

Agnes Odella Smith was united in holy matrimony on February 11, 1931, to the late Rev. John Wesley Holland, also of Cooksville. Out of this union four children were born: the late John W. Holland, Jr., who was a retired Correctional Officer for the State of Maryland; Emerson L. Holland, a retired Air Force Officer; Josephine Holland Dotson, a retired school principal, and Marcella Amelia Holland, a Judge on the Circuit Court for Baltimore City.

The Hollands believed in team parenting. Their first three children were raised in a log cabin, Josephine having been born there. As a young mother, she was called upon to watch over her younger brother, Paul, and younger sister, Harriet, in addition to her young son, John, Jr. She tells many stories of taking the "switch" to or disciplining all three. As her children and the other children in that "village" community soon learned, Agnes Holland did not "spare the rod." But that was the nature of life in general in that small town, for all of the parents in Cooksville made sure that all of the children in their community were safe and well behaved. They raised their children to live by the "Golden Rule."

In addition to cleaning and caring for children, Agnes enjoyed sewing, crocheting, and making quilts. She made dresses for her daughter, Josephine, out of feed bags, and afghans for her children and other family members and friends. She also has a collection of salt and pepper shakers from various places around the country and world, supplied mostly from her late husband and her daughters' travels.

Agnes Odella Holland has been involved in church activities since she was a young child. Her parents took her to Mt. Gregory Methodist Church at an early age. As a young adult, she and her late husband served in many different offices of that church. In the early 40's, she and her late husband joined Full Gospel Tabernacle Church in Catonsville, Maryland. While at Full Gospel Tabernacle, the late Rev. John Wesley Holland was ordained into the ministry and later served as pastor of this church until his death in 1987. The late Rev. Holland helped to build Full Gospel Tabernacle and often served as plumber, electrician, and repairman. Mr. Holland made sure he and the other workers had food and cool drinks during the building phase. She and her late husband worked together as a team to keep the church going. The church's name was changed to Full Gospel Baptist Church in September, 1987.

Agnes Holland is currently a member of Full Gospel Baptist Church. She has served on many committees and served as communion steward for many years. She also served on the Research Circle, Women's Group, and served as custodian of the building, when they could not find anyone else to do the job. Agnes Holland now has the distinctive title of "Mother of the Church." She celebrated her 90th birthday on June 4, 2001.

ORAL HISTORY

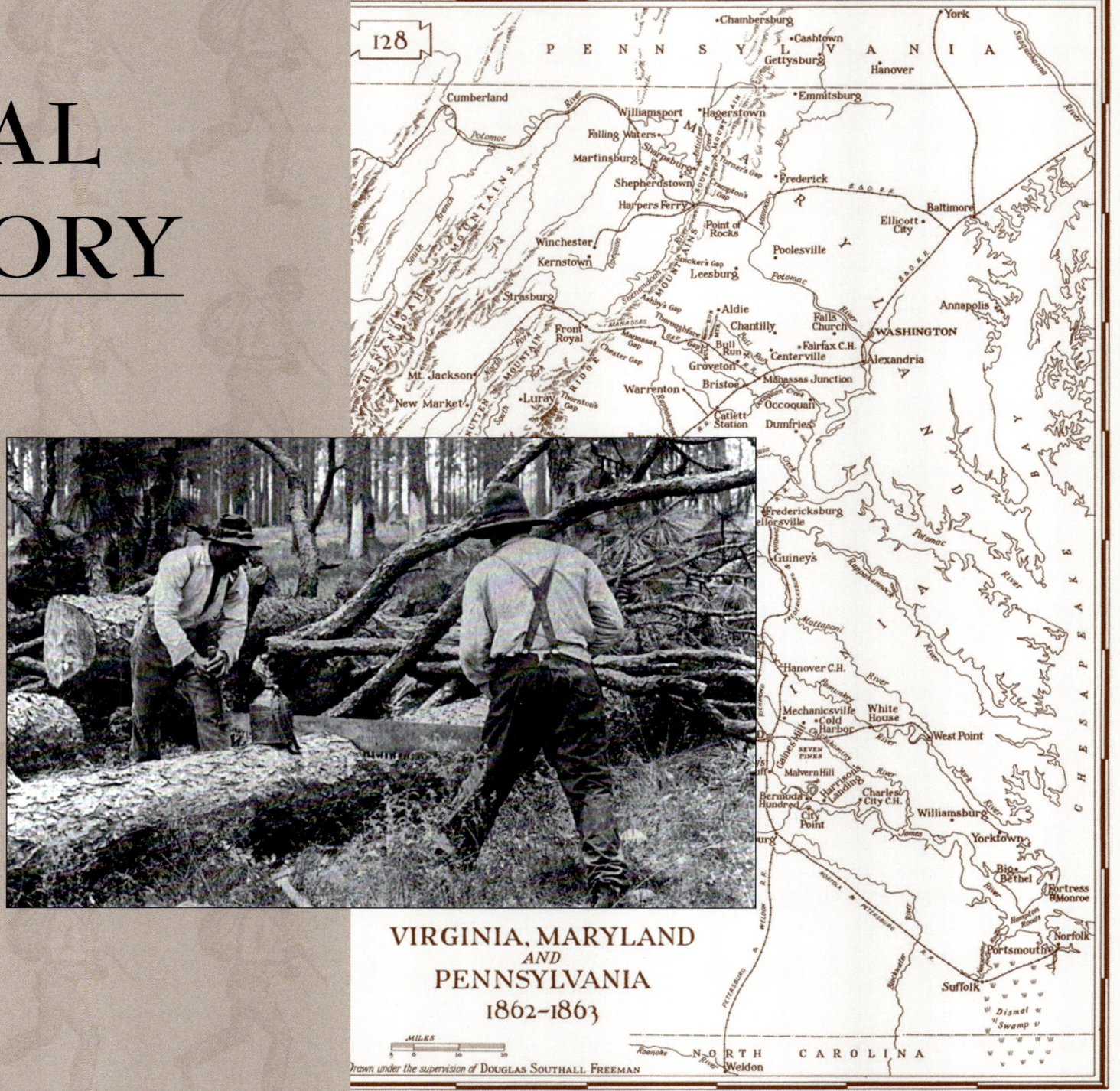

EARL LEVY 1899 – 1993

Mr. Earl Levy was the great-grandson of a slave named Dan or Benjamin Snell, and remembered being born and raised in the log cabin built by his ancestors. The cabin was built in the 1860's. Mr. Snell was given eight acres of woodland on which was built the two-story cabin. Benjamin Snell is buried in the Emily plot a few yards from the log cabin.

"He was a good slave (Benjamin Snell) and after he was free, they let him stay in the quarters. It was cold in the winter, they didn't have but a wood stove and a big fireplace…a big log fireplace you could lay your logs in, and, a iron hook you could hang a pot for slaves to cook. We had a summer kitchen off from the house to keep it from being too hot. But, in the wintertime, you go to bed in the heat… warm, but get up the cold. Water would sometimes be frozen in the buckets. You kept warm 'cause they had a big old feather mattress. They had two mattresses. In the summertime they had a straw mattress and put that on the top to keep you cool.

Now you hear them talking about cutting down trees—it would be great big trees. They would lift them on ox carts, these big men, five or six to a log, didn't care how big it was, you had to lift it up. If you couldn't come up with your end, he (slave-owner) be standing there with his whip—that blacksnake whip. They always carried it on their backs and they cut you with that whip if you couldn't lift up your end.

Everybody wasn't set free at one time. They gave you a pass—those that was free. They gave you a card with your height and scar or whatever you had on your hand, your weight, for when you were caught out. You had to show that!

This man pays so much for you…and they use to take you to a place called Peace Cross, down next to Washington. They use to have it every Monday morning and auction them off like they do cattle or hogs. They load you on the ship, and when the boat pulled off they be waving their hands and never see them no more. Send them to another plantation."

This interview with Earl Levy was produced by Cable Eight, Howard Community College, Howard County Branch of NAACP and Howard County Government.

ORAL HISTORY 99

An interview with Mrs. Sadie Fields on July 31, 2001 at her home in Howard County

BY LAURENCE HURST

HURST   First Mrs. Fields, let's talk about your early life and growing up in Howard County. When were you born?

FIELDS   I was born December 23, 1917.

HURST   And your mother and father's name?

FIELDS   My mother's name was Sadie Emma Jackson, and my father's name was James Edward Snell.

HURST   What do you remember most about your mom and dad and growing up?

FIELDS   It was fun and beautiful, they raised me, and we had a nice life. Seven brothers, and I had only two sisters.

HURST   Did your family always live in the Elkridge area?

FIELDS   Yes, in a way of speaking.

HURST   Where did your mother and father come from?

FIELDS   My father came from Harper's Ferry and my mother came from right around here in the Elkridge area.

HURST   What kind of work did your mother do?

FIELDS   My mother used to go out housekeeping; she used to get up in the morning, get the children straightened out for school, when we return from school, if we were having chicken for dinner, she would catch and clean the chicken. She was a woman who was willing to take care of her children.

HURST   And your father, what type of work did he do?

FIELDS   Well, he had a lot of relatives around here, and still do, who all got together and would say to one another: we going to cut down a tree today, and about twelve or thirteen men would all work together. If one of them had to make a big well, the man who didn't mind fixing the well had to go down the well and make the well high. The men who liked to take care of the pigs would all work together. All my people on my father's side were willing to work together whatever the job was. My mother was housekeeper, all she had to say was one word and we knew what she was talking about. Go to school, be back from school at twelve o'clock, get your lunch and go back to school for your education. In the evening you come home and you would sit and talk in the evening about different things amongst each other. My father would be sitting there because my mother had other things to do. Baking and boiling—ever heard of that? My mother had to do other things while my father was sitting there listening to us—baking and boiling. Baking bread.

HURST   Can you tell me something about the pictures on the wall?

FIELDS   This one is my father. I was proud of him. He was a Snell. The Snells and the Blackstones it seems they were a bunch of people who worked together. They weren't all related to one another. "I'm gonna kill my pig tonight, this evening, you coming down, Ed? Yea, I'll be down there, I'll be down there." And if my mother needed an extra dip of tea she would say run down there and tell Aunt Maude to send me a little bit of tea; I don't have any tea here. We would walk from the hill down by the church and wouldn't stop and play no form or fashion. We got what we want and the elderly people would peep out the window at you.

"Get what momma told you to get and run on home. You sure you didn't eat none." You had to get back home in time to go to the store to get momma a little something at the store. The store wasn't too far from here. We'd walk to the store, walk back from the store. We were well-trained children. We were well known in the community. My father, he was well known around here in Meadowridge and he said those men that he worked with and traveled with were his first cousins. They believed in going to church too. My mother was a great church worker. My father, he liked to work at the church, but men were different in those days. That's the way life was. It was a beautiful life.

HURST   How many years did you go to school?

FIELDS I completed (7th grade). That was all they had.

HURST   What was going to school like? What school did you attend?

FIELDS The school was right up the road here. It was called Meadowridge Colored School. My teacher got off the bus at Meadowridge Road and walked up Meadowridge Road to school. She was from Baltimore. Her name was Mamie G. McGruder

HURST   What year did you get married?

FIELDS In 1936.

HURST   How did you meet your husband?

FIELDS Those were the good old days (laughs). For one thing, my husband he had a job in lower Elkridge, and I must have been an awful cute girl 'cause he always made a special trip to my mother's house with a bag of ice for me. We had ice boxes then, we didn't have a refrigerator. My husband's name was William Henry Fields. He was an iceman. He would bring the ice up to my mother's house. We had a porch then. He would come and father would be reared back looking at him and if he had turned around to look at my mother, my father would look as if he could have shot him. That's how my father looked at him—"You just come put ice in there and go on about your business." This went on for so long I got tired of it myself. Willie would tell me about the beautiful kinfolks he had down in the country. I said, "Do you think they'll like me?" And he said, "Yea Come on, I'm going to take you down there." I had to go down there; I had to ask Poppa and Momma. Momma, will you please ask Poppa. Momma said, "I will get it straightened out." When the time came to go, Momma got some of those turnip tops and she said, "You take this with you, and when you get to that lady's house where you going, you give this to her 'cause she would love it." All the way to Laurel, I kept thinking. Willie was right beside me; he was driving. All those people down Laurel jumped on me because I had this little package. I got so tickled, I said, "Is that how they act?" And Willie said, "Yea, we going to have a nice time." Honey I spent the night down there with him. I spent the night with him and from that day to this I ain't had no trouble out of him.

ORAL HISTORY 101

HURST   Did your husband build this house?

FIELDS   Yes, my husband built this house by himself. He built those three rooms back there by himself and then eventually he built this room. And we had a store; we sold bread, kerosene, and candy for the kids.

HURST   How many children do you have?

FIELDS   I have five daughters: Marion Neeley, Levina McGee, Taminika Odinga, Gertrude Belt, and Karen Manning is the baby, and two boys, William Henry Fields, Jr., and Frederick Marcel Fields.

HURST   Who was the neighborhood doctor?

FIELDS   Dr. Bumguard. He was good. He helped me to born my babies at home, all except Taminika. He always took time to come. He would sit and read the paper.

HURST   Did you have any family with military experience?

FIELDS   Junior. His name is William Henry Fields like his daddy, and he went in the Air Force.

HURST   I see you have a beautiful garden out here.

FIELDS   I have always liked flowers. My whole family loved flowers, my father and my mother. My mother had trees she would trim and my father was always behind her.

HURST   Did you preserve food, canned foods?

FIELDS   Canning! That was my job when I first married my husband. Oh, that went on for about ten years 'til my husband got in my way—he liked to cook.

HURST   And hobbies, did you like to sew?

FIELDS   Yes, I sewed. I sewed at night when they was sleep. My husband would come down in the morning and say, "What is that?" The children were so fond of their father. "Daddy, I don't like that thing Momma made." Then he would get after me—"They don't like it, don't put it there for them."

HURST   What church are you a member of and do you sing?

FIELDS   I am a member of the Senior Choir at St. Stephens AME Church. I was a great Usher in my church. I was the President of the Usher Board. I still am on the Usher Board.

HURST   How did you travel?

FIELDS   Walked.

HURST   Did you have white neighbors? What was the relationship like?

FIELDS   My momma worked for the white people. We didn't have any white neighbors, none of that. My momma was a workingwoman; my father was a workingman.

HURST   Did you ever experience or know of any racial tension with whites?

FIELDS   No, we were all social people. There was this woman, she was a colored woman and her husband was a white man. We used to call him "Mr. Whiteman."

An interview with Mrs. Mildred Myers on July 12, 2001 in Highland, Maryland

BY LAURENCE HURST

HURST   Hello, I'm Laurence Hurst and first of all I want to ask you a little about your life and family. When and where were you born?

MYERS   April 9, 1916 in Clarksville.

HURST   And your mother and father's name?

MYERS   My mother was named Laura Wilson and my father was named Kenneth Wilson and they were from right here in Howard County.

HURST   What do you remember most about your mom?

MYERS   Well, she was the type of a person, she liked to have a lot of fun. I know that she was more different than my dad. She always went to church and so did dad. Both of them sang on the choir in the church, and a lot of other organizations in the church both of them was involved in.

HURST   How many bothers and sisters do you have?

MYERS   I didn't have any brothers, it was just four girls. I was the oldest, and then Janie, then Sarah, and then my baby sister Earlene lives next door and we are the only two living now.

HURST   What do you remember most about growing up as a little girl here in Howard County?

MYERS   Well, mostly what I know about family. We always had to go to church, and of course we had to make sure that we went to school, which I loved to go to. When I couldn't go to school I used to always cry. We went to a little school up here called Highland Elementary and we had to walk all the way from Clarksville to Highland.

HURST   How long was the walk?

MYERS   It was a long way and sometimes we were so cold that when we got to school we didn't know whether we had hands or feet.

HURST   What was school life like as a young girl in this area? You mentioned that you had to walk there and that it was cold, but what was it like as far as instruction? What type of subjects did you have?

MYERS   Well, school as far as I'm concerned wasn't too good. I was very smart in school, always did good, but we always got the books that was left over from the white children.

Sometimes I remember sitting in school trying to find a subject and when you opened the book half the leaves were on the floor. But I can say that what I had to go through I am proud of, 'cause I was determined to learn. What I had, I used it for my advantage.

HURST What was your relationship like with whites?

MYERS Well, it wasn't good. When we went to school, we went in the opposite direction than the white students. All of us walked, we would meet practically every day and would have a big fight, a big stone fight before we got to school because of the names that they would call us. I remember one day that my sister and I was walking alone, we missed the other bunch and this bunch of white boys met us and we were very afraid. They called us everything. It was very cold that morning and we had on these little nubie hats. They took our nubie hats off our heads and threw them over in the cornfield. We cried all the way to school but the next morning our mother walked out with us and of course they didn't bother us that morning. When we got with our group they really didn't bother us because we had some big boys. They had some big boys too but our boys always could beat them and they were afraid.

HURST Do you remember any of your teachers?

MYERS The first teacher I had was Mrs. Burris and the next teacher was Dola White. They were the only two teachers I had. I went to Mrs. Burris one year. I was in the first grade when she came here and then Dola White came and she stayed here until I got out of school. Seventh grade was as far as we went because we didn't have any high school for Black children then. We had our little graduation exercise in Ellicott City. After that, I did go to night school for a while taking up Math and English. That school was the old elementary school in Guilford. We had a teacher to come there and I went there for a while but eventually that closed because of funds.

HURST What church did you attend?

MYERS Right up here (Highland)—Hopkins United Methodist Church, we always went there.

HURST What about your other family members; did they always attend that church, too?

MYERS Yes! They always attended that church.

HURST From your experience, what do you know of some of your early family members that moved into this area?

MYERS Well, from what my mother and father have told me, they all lived in this area. I had a grandfather and grandmother that lived up here on the hill somewhere but the house isn't there anymore.

HURST What was your husband's name and when did you marry?

MYERS His name was William, and we married May 18, 1935.

HURST Did you marry in the church?

MYERS No, we just went to the minister (laughs).

HURST How did you meet your husband?

MYERS Well, I think I met him at a ballgame.

HURST How many children do you have?

MYERS Seven—five girls and two boys, one boy is deceased.

HURST What was life like for a young married couple in Howard County? What were your prospects for the future and what kinds of things did you want to do?

MYERS   Well, I must say, it was good. I was a very quiet person. My friends always say they don't know how I got a husband, but we married. He was a workaholic—I can say that. My kids didn't ever need for anything. He always took care of us. They never went hungry 'cause we raised chickens, we raised pigs, and I always would can everything that grew on a stem. We had a very large garden.

HURST   As far as your garden, did you sell any of the produce, or trade?

MYERS   No, I did not. We gave a lot of it away to other people when we had too much but we never sold anything.

HURST   What kind of work did your husband do?

MYERS   Well, he drove the school bus in the day (I tell you he was a workaholic) and he worked over to Johns Hopkins physics lab at night in Laurel.

HURST   How was this house built? Did you have to save money and what was the experience like?

MYERS   Well, my husband bought this land. It's two acres here. He paid $200; $100 an acre. At that time we lived in Simpsonville and it was because of my father, Kenneth Wilson, who worked for this white man who sold him two acres that we were able to get this land. This was a pre-fabbed house. He would get off from work in the evenings and come up here and put it together. Now he had the blueprint and I would sit in the yard (laughs) and read off to him the parts that he would have to put together. The men of our church, which they did a lot of it, got together evenings and they came down and helped him to build this house without charging him anything. All he had to do was pay for the material. At that time I don't think we paid over $8,000 for this home.

HURST   And you raised your children here?

MYERS   I raised some. I think when we moved here three of them was married, but the others came here and of course I sent them to high school in Glenelg.

HURST   How long have you been living here now?

MYERS   Thirty-five years.

HURST   What was the area like when you first moved here? It must have been very rural back then.

ORAL HISTORY 105

MYERS   It was very, very rural. It wasn't any houses on Highland Road. From my church up here down to Highland was all a wooded area. You could walk from my church all the way down to the Highland store and the trees met each other over the road. It was a dirt road and you could walk all the way to Highland in the shade without even getting in the sun.

HURST   Who were some of the earlier doctors in this area and how did they give service?

MYERS   My first doctor was Dr. Nicholas. My second doctor was Dr. Whittaker and my doctor now is Dr. Evelyn Jackson. Dr. Nicholas, the first doctor, would come to your house. Dr. Whittaker would come depending on how bad the patient was. But now I have Dr. Jackson and that is a different situation.

HURST   Did the same doctors perform child birthing and childcare?

MYERS   No, they didn't. Three of my children were born in Baltimore at the hospital. One was born at the Montgomery County General Hospital and the others were born at home.

HURST   How was clothing acquired? Did you shop for them or make them?

MYERS   For my children, I did a lot of sewing. Other than that we always went to Ellicott City. Sometimes we got into Baltimore, but very seldom. I always had the in-laws and they were larger than I, and I always was given something. I was very blessed with that. But as far as the children were concerned, I made all of their dresses and everything, but not for my boys. When the girls got older they would say, "I'm not going to church with a dress you made." But when they were smaller they didn't pay any attention to that, they wore them.

HURST   Generally speaking about Howard County, what do you like most about living in this area?

MYERS   Well, this is the only area that I have lived in and it's hard for me to describe. I love it here I can say that.

HURST   Why, for what reasons?

MYERS   I guess because I have lived here all my life.

An interview with Rev. Samuel Moore on August 2, 2001 at his home in Jessup, Maryland

BY LAURENCE HURST

HURST Rev. Moore, I understand you are a native of Howard County. Can you tell us a little about what it was like growing up in the Guilford/Jessup area of the county?

MOORE Well, when I began to know, and to learn, and to become acquainted with, and became old enough to know how things were happening in the county, I remember there was a lot of segregation. That's the first thing. I can remember when you couldn't go into Savage without meeting a lot of opposition. They didn't like blacks in Savage. My father worked here in helping to build the mill in Savage.

HURST What schools did you attend?

MOORE In Baltimore, I went to school on Saratoga and Mount Street. I think that school is no longer there now. I don't recall the name. Then too, I attended a school in Wilson Park in the Govans area of Baltimore in the lower grades, in the first and second grades. We used to live on St. George's Avenue, not too far from the college. We moved from there back in the county. That's where I finished the seventh grade. They only went to seventh grade out here. Not long after that I worked in Washington, DC for a number of years over at the Pentagon and over at the Naval Hospital in Bethesda. I worked in the shipyard in the forties during the wartime. After that, I became a member of the church at First Baptist Church here in Guilford. After becoming a member of First Baptist I went into the Ministry. I was called to the Ministry, and I went, then I finished my studies I went to Baptist Center School of Religion for four years and received the Certificate for the study in Theology. After that, I enrolled in Marsh College School of Religion. It was an extension from Sumter, SC. I only could make two years of that. After studying there for a while, they called me to the church here in Elkridge in 1960. Prior to that I served two years in the absence of the pastor who took sick and I've been there every since. That was in Elkridge on Church Avenue. That church is no longer there. It was named Unity Baptist.

HURST What inspired you to go into Ministry as a profession?

MOORE My mother and father. My father was a minister for one thing and my mother was a devoted Christian. I had uncles and a lot of my family were very religious people and I guess that helped to inspire me to go into the ministry. After feeling the call, I felt the call about 1947, but it wasn't until 1950-51 that I got into the Ministry. I was licensed here at First Baptist of Guilford under the Rev. Charles Jackson. I graduated from the Baptist School of Religion in 1956 and was ordained in 1960. That's when I was called to pastor at Unity Baptist.

HURST Rev. Moore, when were you born?

MOORE November 21, 1919. Right here in Howard County.

HURST Tell me a little about your mother and father.

MOORE My mother came from Ellicott City. My father was born here in Colesville. That's here in Howard County, it's near Laurel and he was a preacher, a minister. Their names were Emma Jane and Randolph Moore. He was a minister and she was a devoted Christian and it was seventeen of us.

HURST What was life like growing up with a large family like that?

MOORE They always made ends meet. My dad used to do a lot of farming and he worked in private families as a butler. He would come home on the weekends and then go back. We would have to do the gardening, the older brothers used to have to take care of the farm and raising stuff, that type of thing.

HURST So you had a farm also?

MOORE Yes, a small farm.

HURST Did your father and mother ever speak about their educational experience?

MOORE Not really. My mother went to the Ellicott City School in one of those old buildings up there.

HURST Did they ever mention the issue of slavery?

MOORE Not really, my grandmother was an Indian. They lived in Bacontown, Maryland (right up above Laurel) and we had pictures of her, but they got lost. I didn't know too much about grandfather, but he lived in Colesville in Howard County.

HURST How did you meet your wife?

MOORE I think I met her one day with some other young women that my brother was friends with. She's from Glen Burnie, Queenstown, and after meeting we went out. I think she was in Bates High School, Annapolis. That's how I met her. I met her through another couple at the school.

HURST And your wife's name?

MOORE Mary Beaulah Moore—she was a Gaither.

HURST How many children did you have from this union?

MOORE Nine. Samuel, Charles, Frankie, Arthena, Stanley, Cynthia, Phillip, Marie, and Valerie.

HURST Let's talk about the house that you stayed in when you were a child. Did your father build it?

MOORE No. My father never built any houses at all. All we did was move from place to place. One house was on Mission Road. We moved out of Highridge and we moved up here on Mission Road. We moved to a place in Annapolis Junction. We moved from Annapolis Junction to Mission

Road, to Baltimore City and then to Baltimore County in Govans or Wilson Park. We moved from Wilson Park back to Baltimore City and from Baltimore City back into Howard County.

HURST When you came back to the area what was it like as a community?

MOORE There wasn't anything in this area. From Route 1, on the left hand side coming up Guilford Road about a half mile, two or three blocks off of Route 1 it was some houses to the left, only two. They were way back off the road. One of them my older brother lived in and when we came from Baltimore City the younger ones stayed with his family until we got settled out here; mother and father came out here too. This road was completely vacant, nothing but woods, nothing out here. It was a farm on the left hand side and that house sat way back. From there, it was a school (Guilford Elementary School) on the right hand side here on Mission Road. From there it wasn't anything, no houses nowhere else until you got up to Guilford and Oakland Mills. It was a big store there and it sold all kinds of things, everything.

HURST When you moved here what was it like to acquire land or property? Was it difficult?

MOORE No. I bought this property off of a guy who had bought it and he sold it to us. My brother John, who lived next door, had already bought some property here and also a brother that lived on this side, Leonard, he had already bought some. Now, both of them are deceased. This piece of property, the guy who bought it didn't do anything with it for a while. It was all woods and everything and I approached him and asked him if he wanted to sell it, and he sold it to me. There were two lots together. He sold one lot at a time. There was a time back in my early days, I would cut logs off of this land and haul them to the sawmill. They would haul the lumber to Hebbsville in Baltimore County. The guy that owned that mill owned all this property. He also owned the mill on Windsor Mill Road. He was a German.

HURST Was there a church in the area also?

MOORE Yes. It was an old church up to Carter's lane across from the elementary school. Across from the elementary school there was a store and the First Baptist Church of Guilford. That's where I was ordained. That's where our membership started, right there. Down this way across Route 1 is Asbury, a Methodist church. My parents attended that church and I went there as a small boy to Sunday school.

HURST Who was the doctor that served this neighborhood and what services were available?

MOORE We used Dr. Shipley and Dr. Warren. Dr. Shipley was here in Savage and Dr. Warren was in Laurel. They were both white doctors. At Dr. Shipley's office everybody sat in the same room. At Dr. Warren's office, blacks sat in a little area and whites sat in another area. Dr. Shipley would give you a pill and tell you to go ahead. He did a lot of work in our family, did a lot of delivering babies.

HURST   Can you name some of the families you were associated with?

MOORE   Yes. When you got into Guilford on Oakland Mills Road there was a black community there. The Hardings, the Carters—it was quite a number of blacks in that area and one or two whites. The whites were very friendly who lived there and very helpful. If you needed anything they would help. This wasn't Guilford Road at this time, it was called Route 32.

HURST   Did you have any hobbies or special interests growing up?

MOORE   I used to love to dance and I got trophies for dancing. I joined the church at 45 and after that I put everything down.

HURST   What did kids and people do for recreation?

MOORE   Play ball.

HURST   Any other special games?

MOORE   Yea! Shooting marbles was a big thing back in those days and horseshoes.

HURST   What types of early organizations outside of church for African Americans were available to join?

MOORE   One was the Masons. You could join those types of organizations. There were also organizations extended from the churches, such as the Odd Fellows.

HURST   What type of discrimination/segregation was present in a rural area like this?

MOORE   They just wouldn't allow you to come where they were. If they had some activity in their school or something like that, you just weren't supposed to be there.

HURST   Were you ever involved in any political activity?

MOORE   We've voted since I don't know when; we've always voted, but I never campaigned for anyone in particular. Politicians would come to different places in the county and we would go to hear what they had to say and if we felt good about them we would let them know they had our vote.

HURST   Can you share some of your experiences with the Ku Klux Klan?

MOORE   I remember this and I never will forget it. I think it was the early 1960's. Someone dropped dynamite or a bomb or something in the yard. That's when we were doing a lot of protesting for the right to go to schools, and to sit down in the various lunchrooms. It was really, really hot up this road because this community was always a community that was fighting for what's right. We had those kind of young men here who moved in the county and were fighters. They inspired the other people here in the county to join in with them. For instance, we had people in the community like Morris Woodson and Elhart Flurry, Silas Craft and Mrs. Aileen Moore. They were fighters and people from Elkridge, the Hawkins family and quite a number of people around here. Rev. Arter and Rev. John Holland, they were in the midst of it. During that time we were fighting for rights and during that time somebody threw a bomb in this yard. I don't know if it was meant for me or meant for somebody else. We got a lot of things done in Elkridge that was closed against blacks, especially for using public facilities, but we broke that up. It was a lot of fighting going on for what belonged to us.

HURST   Let's go back to church life. Can you tell us about the early churches in this area and their interaction with each other?

MOORE   We visited churches all around in this community. Baptists and Methodists; up to Hopkins, Highland and Simpsonville, over to Highridge and Elkridge, Asbury and Ellicott City, and Catonsville. We had fellowship with all those churches. Now its two Baptist churches in this community, one at Waterloo and one in Guilford. The rest are Methodists—Asbury, Hopkins, Altholton, and Ellicott City. Since I've been in the Ministry serving as Pastor at Elkridge, we've had fellowship with white churches there. We've spoken in several white churches and they have been to our church. Now that was in the 1960's when we had that fellowship. We spoke at Grace Episcopal, and we spoke at the Baptist church in Elkridge and both of those ministers visited us and spoke at our congregations.

HURST   And there was no tension from the community?

MOORE   No. It may have been but we never recognized any of it. It could have been amongst some of the members. During the time of the terrible flood in 1972 Agnes came through and practically destroyed Unity Baptist, which was on Church Avenue. The water came up to the eves of the building. You could only see the top, and the roof. It was a real nice church inside. We had just done some renovations there, we had just put in new pews and a new addition. When we went there we pulled all those big cement things they had in the bottom to hold it up, took them out and put regular high beams in, we put a new floor in and a side entrance and made it real nice. Then Agnes came and wiped us out, but the following Sunday we had service in the basement. It devastated us but we got a lot of assistance from various churches in the area, white and black. There was a Methodist church there in the area that had a very fine white minister; they gave us a lot of money and a lot of assistance. They fixed sandwiches for us while we were trying to clean the church up and get it back into shape. The church was Grace Episcopal up here on Route 1; those people helped us and a lot of white folks helped us at that time. Trinity Episcopal helped also. The minister was Randal Pratt from Melville. Hurricane Eloise came by and got us too. People had built homes down in Elkridge Landing and they didn't want to leave. They said that in this area boats used to come up in there and take tobacco and pigs to Baltimore. They were reluctant to move when Eloise came through and devastated us again. So they made up their minds that they were ready to move. They had boats and everything down there and the fire department to move everybody out. Unity Baptist was on Church Avenue. The church was about a mile behind Furnace Inn.

Today Rev. Moore's church is on Montgomery Road near the bank.
It's the same name – Unity Baptist.
We didn't move too far from the area so we didn't lose the identity.

CONCLUSION

"Though I am more closely connected
and identified with
one class of outraged,
oppressed and enslaved people,
I cannot allow myself
to be insensible
to the wrongs and sufferings
of any part of
the great family
of man.
I am not only an American slave,
but a man and, as such,
am bound to use my powers
for the welfare of the
whole human brotherhood."[1]

– Frederick Douglass, 1846

POST EMANCIPATION LITERATURE 1863–1899

"On New Year's Eve, 1862, black people all over the nation gathered to sing and pray as they waited for the hour of midnight to bring into law the Emancipation Proclamation."[2] The following song was sung several times:

> O, go down Moses
> Way down in Egypt's land
> Tell King Pharaoh
> To let my people go.[3]

112   SEEKING FREEDOM

Throughout history, people continue to wonder at the success of the Underground Railroad Movement (UGR). The mystery of the UGR is the fact that the Movement peaked during the time that the institution of slavery was both legal and profitable and had to be preserved at all costs. Historians claim well over 100,000 slave fugitives escaped to freedom by means of the Underground Railroad.

Several key factors emerge from the UGR story: many significant contributions were made by slaves or African Americans to the economic development of the country and the county; cooperation between the races was required for the UGR Movement to succeed; and moreover, people in bondage would risk their lives for the life of joy and freedom promised in both the Declaration of Independence and the United States of America's Constitution.

The fact that slavery existed in Howard County attests that African Americans contributed to the county's development and its richness. The fact that the Underground Railroad ran throughout the county shows that Howard Countians from different religious and racial backgrounds risked their lives for their freedom and that of their fellow men. *Seeking Freedom: A History of the Underground Railroad in Howard County, Maryland* is written to keep the "freedom" story alive and to highlight the contributions African Americans have made to this county. To assure that "freedom" stays alive for generations to come, we make the following recommendations:

☞ That there be a historic marker program to include all major underground railroad sites in Howard County.

☞ That a school curriculum, educational projects, exhibits, and tours be developed and/or undertaken from this research project.

☞ That a state marker be erected for Harriet Tubman Lane (formerly Freetown Road).

☞ That other neighboring counties research and publish underground railroad related materials.

REFERENCES

1. *The Life and Times of Frederick Douglass*, Letter from Montrose Scotland, to William Lloyd Garrison, American abolitionist leader, 26 February 1846, Foner, Vol 1, p. 138.

2. *The Social Implications of Early Negro Music*, Edited by Bernard Katz, Anno Press, New York, 1969.

3. Ibid.

BIBLIOGRAPY

PRIMARY SOURCES

United States Census of 1860, Howard County Historical Society, Ellicott City, Maryland. (microfilm)

Maryland Historic Sites Inventory, Howard County Historical Society, Ellicott City, Maryland

MAGAZINES AND PERIODICALS:

Carroll, Kenneth, L. "Voices of Protest: Eastern Shore Abolition Society, 1790–1820," *Maryland Historical Magazine*, Vol. 184, No. 4, Pg. 319

Brown, Christopher, C. "Maryland's First Political Convention By and For Its Colored People," *Maryland Historical Society*, Vol. 88, No. 3, Fall 1993, Pg. 324.

Quarles, Benjamin, "Freedom Fettered": Blacks in the Constitutional Era in Maryland, 1776–1810, An Introduction, *Maryland Historical Magazine*, Vol. 84, No. 4, Winter 1989, Pg. 99.

Guy, Anita Aidt, "The Maryland Abolition Society and the Promotion of the Ideals of the New Nation," *Maryland Historical Magazine*, Vol. 84, No. 4, Winter 1989.

BOOKS

Bedini, Silvio A. *The Life of Benjamin Banneker: The Definitive Biography of the First Black Man of Science*, New York: Charles Scribner's Sons, 1972.

Calderhead, William L., *Thomas Carney: Unsung Soldier of the American Revolution*, Baltimore: Maryland Historical Society, Winter, 1989.

Cohen, Anthony, *The Underground Railroad in Montgomery County, Maryland: A History and Driving Guide*, Montgomery County, Maryland: Montgomery County Historical Society, 1995.

Cornelison, Craft and Lillie Price, *History of Blacks in Howard County*, Howard County, Maryland: NAACP, 1986.

Holland, Celia M., *Old Homes and Families of Howard County Maryland*, Privately Printed, 1987.

Stein, Charles Francis, Jr., *Origin and History of Howard County*, Baltimore, Maryland: Author in cooperation with Howard County Historical Society, 1972.

Voris, Helen P., *Elkridge: Where It All Began*, Elkridge, Maryland: Privately Printed, 2000.

	DATE DUE	

973.7 SEE   Seeking freedom